Lean Teaching

A Guide to Becoming a Better Teacher

Bob Emiliani, Ph.D.

The CLBM, LLC
Wethersfield, Conn.

© 2015 by M.L. "Bob" Emiliani

Except as permitted under U.S. Copyright law, no part of this publication may be reprinted, reproduced, distributed, transmitted, or utilized in any form or by any electronic, mechanical, or other means, now known or hereafter invented, including photocopying, microfilming, and recording, or in any information storage or retrieval system, without the prior written permission from the publisher. Direct permission requests to: bob@bobemiliani.com

Reasonable efforts have been made to publish reliable information, but author and publisher cannot assume responsibility for the validity of all materials or the consequences of their use. This book contains content from some of the author's previous publications.

Lean Teaching: A Guide to Becoming a Better Teacher / M.L. "Bob" Emiliani

Cover design and illustrations by Bob Emiliani. Appendix III graphs by Kamna Tiwari.

ISBN-13: 978-0-9898631-1-7

Library of Congress Control Number: 2015908482

1. Teaching 2. Higher Education 3. Lean Management
4. Leadership 5. Business 6. Non-profit

First Edition: June 2015

Published previously as an e-book titled: *The Lean Professor: Become a Better Teacher Using Lean Principles and Practices* (2013). This print version is revised and expanded.

Published by The CLBM, LLC, Wethersfield, Connecticut, USA

Manufactured using digital print-on-demand technology.

For my students.

Together we learn and improve.

CONTENTS

Preface		vii
Introduction		1
Chapter 1	What Is Lean Management?	13
Chapter 2	Unforced Teaching Errors	31
Chapter 3	Teaching Process Improvements	39
Chapter 4	Outcomes Assessment	51
Chapter 5	More Teaching Process Improvements	61
Chapter 6	More Outcomes Assessment	87
Chapter 7	Closing Remarks	99
Appendix I	Imaginary Customers	107
Appendix II	Questions and Answers	109
Appendix III	Teaching Survey Findings	117
About the Author		131

Preface

I would like to begin by telling clearing up some confusion in terminology that may exist regarding the terms "teaching Lean" and "Lean teaching." Teaching Lean means to teaching the subject Lean management and related topics to students so that they may advance their practice of management. Lean teaching means to apply the principles and practices of Lean management to teaching. Specifically, the design and delivery of courses.

Lean Teaching shares with you what I have learned by applying Lean principles and practices to teaching over the 16 years that I have been a professor in academia. As far as I can tell, I am the first to do this. This is largely due the specific training and daily practice in Lean management that I was exposed to when I worked in industry prior to joining academia. I want to share this because I believe other professors will benefit greatly by learning a different way of thinking about teaching and how to improve their courses.

This book is a heartfelt effort to help faculty correctly understand Lean principles and practices and to begin applying them to their own courses [1]. A motivation for wanting to do so is to recognize that academic courses and programs are a principal source of value creation in higher education. Administrative processes, while not a source of value creation, do shape students perceptions of value. They too are important processes that can be greatly improved using Lean principles and practices.

It is my hope that this book will inspire faculty to learn a different way to improve teaching, one that I have found results in higher levels of student engagement and better learning outcomes. I am confident that if practiced widely by all faculty in a college or university, it can also result in higher completion rates and post-graduation student success. All of this can be achieved in non-zero-sum (win-win) ways that benefit every stakeholder.

Upon completing my Ph.D. in Engineering from Brown University in 1988, I interviewed for positions in both academia and in industry. The jobs in academia were less compelling to me than the jobs in industry. Ultimately, I accepted a position in the materials engineering department at Pratt & Whitney, a unit of United Technologies Corporation.

I worked on various research and development (R&D) projects for about seven years, fully utilizing the degrees for which I was educated. My managers recognized my work as high quality, but I had doubts about doing R&D work for another 25 years. It seemed like it would get increasingly boring as the years passed. Plus, I wanted to work on something that had more immediate outcomes, rather than work on projects that might come to fruition decades into the future.

I had conversations with a colleague who had worked in manufacturing, and he urged me to meet with an executive to talk about job opportunities there. So, I did, and was excited about what I had heard. Pratt & Whitney's manufacturing operations was undergoing great change and seeking to diversify its management team. Soon, I was offered a job as a business unit manager in manufacturing, which I accepted in the summer of 1994 [2].

The big change in Pratt & Whitney's manufacturing operations was the presence of consultants from Japan who were teaching us how to improve processes to achieve consistently better outcomes. They were teaching us Toyota production system (TPS) principles and methods [3, 4], which was also known more narrowly as "Lean production" at that time [5, 6]. Lean is now recognized as a comprehensive system of progressive management practice, and is termed "Lean management."

I participated in my first kaizen (a process improvement activity) within a few weeks after starting my new job in July 1994. The term "kaizen" was familiar to me because a year or so earlier I had read Masaaki Imai's book *Kaizen: The Key to Japan's Competitive Success*. Now, my limited book knowledge was being transformed into deep practical knowledge thanks to the teachings of

Shingijutsu consultants (who were retired industrial engineers from Toyota, Toyoda Gosei, and Isuzu).

Kaizen, led by people who were trained by pioneers of the process improvement method, or who were experts at it, was a life-changing experience for me, and the most fun I ever had at work. We were finally able to think "outside the box" and tap into our individual and collective imaginations about what was possible to achieve. We made wonderful and amazing improvements. I made greater contributions to the company than ever before and I even felt better. I have not been the same since.

It is very important to understand that we could not have made the improvements previously. We did not understand the details of our work processes or what "flow" meant. But, more important, we did not know how to think. Shingijutsu consultants taught us how to think critically at a level that far surpassed how everyone was taught to think in school. At the same time, they taught us how to be creative and spend ideas instead of money to make big improvements.

This experience made it clear to me that in school we are taught to think critically in a rudimentary or low-level way, which is partly why problems persist in organizations for decades. In general, the result of normal educational processes, up to and including doctoral degrees, ranges from sub-critical thinking to critical thinking. Shingijutsu consultants taught us supra-critical thinking. They taught us to question things and see things in ways that nobody had ever done before. It can be summed up this way: Lean thinking is supra-critical (or Xtreme critical) thinking. It is a level of critical thinking that surpasses what is normally taught in school. That is why people who learn Lean well are so annoyed with old ways of understanding and doing things, which are based merely on sub-critical thinking or critical thinking [7].

I recall being asked by a co-worker in late 1994 whether Toyota's production system could be applied to service processes. I said "No, I don't see how you'd do that." Well, I was totally wrong. My narrow view of needing to rapidly improve manufacturing processes to correct chronic cost, delivery, and quality problems prevented me from understanding the bigger picture. That bigger picture was this: All work is part of a process, and all process can be improved – regardless of if it's a manufacturing or service process – to achieve consistently better outcomes. It is true that in some organizations it might be more of a challenge to improve processes, but time and experience has shown that remarkable improvements can be made using supra-critical (Lean) thinking.

While I enjoyed my time in engineering, manufacturing offered huge yet welcomed personal challenges and experiences. The things I learned made me a better engineer and a better businessperson. Learning about progressive Lean management was the kind of experience that comes once in a lifetime and changes the way you see and interact with the world. It instilled in me principles and methods that I could apply to any job to make things better for both people and processes.

Following my work in manufacturing, I was recruited to lead a team in the purchasing department, responsible for the annual procurement of $100 million of machined parts from mostly local suppliers [8]. This was a marvelous opportunity to apply what I had learned about Lean management in manufacturing to supply chains. With a colleague, we worked to teach our first-, second-, and third-tier manufacturing and service suppliers about Lean. In addition, we applied Lean principles and practices to improve internal purchasing processes.

After a successful 12-year career in industry, including three promotions, I decided the time was right to enter academia. My formal education, coupled with practical work experience in three different disciplines (engineering, manufacturing, and supply chain) made me much better qualified to teach at the university level [9].

I accepted a full-time position as a clinical professor in the Lally School of Management and Technology at the Hartford, Conn., campus of Rensselaer Polytechnic Institute (RPI) in 1999. As a result of my experiences learning and applying Lean management at Pratt & Whitney, I could see that the services provided by universities were inadequate to students as well as other stakeholders (such as employers). Both academic processes and administrative processes needed to be improved. I led or participated on various teams to improve administrative processes. I also set out to apply Lean principles and practices to the design and delivery of my courses [10], and organized and led kaizens to improve a Master's degree program [11, 12]. After five years at RPI, I joined Central Connecticut State University (CCSU) as a professor in the School of Engineering and Technology.

This book describes the work that I did, and continue to do today, in applying Lean principles and practices in academia [13], and what other professors can do to improve their teaching processes. It is the application of supra-critical (Lean) thinking, taught to me by Shingijutsu consultants, to teaching.

I do not present myself as an expert or someone who suggests that this is the one best way. Instead, I am simply a teacher who likes to try new things and learn from the resulting experience. To you, I humbly offer the approach and rationale for what I do, and insights into the outcomes achieved. I am ever mindful of the need for additional improvement.

I hope this book will reverse any negative impressions or self-limiting views that faculty may have, such as:

- Lean is just a manufacturing thing.
- All ideas from industry are crap.
- This does not apply to my department.
- My discipline has been taught this way for decades. There is no need to change.
- The way I teach this difficult subject cannot be improved.

The learned are not exempt from learning how to continuously improve their work.

In my view, professors are remiss in their primary duty of educating students if they do not recognize teaching problems and work to make substantive process improvements that students notice.

Many professors do recognize problems and make improvements. Many of those improvements may possess characteristics consistent with Lean principles and practices. However, such improvements may not address the root cause of problems, are limited to what one can do alone, or improvements are not shared with other faculty.

Professors, however, are not alone in their efforts to deliver value to students. Administrators are remiss in their primary duty of managing institutions of higher education (people and processes) if they do not recognize management problems and work to make substantive process improvements. For that, they should read my book, *Lean University: A Guide to Renewal and Prosperity* [14], and Prof. William Balzer's book, *Lean Higher Education: Increasing the Value and Performance of University Processes* [15].

While this book is intended for professors in higher education, it will also be useful for administrators of academic units, including department chairs, deans, provosts, and university presidents. The members of university boards will also benefit from reading this book.

Finally, I hope that this book begins a constructive dialog between faculty within colleges and universities and between colleges and universities on the topic of Lean teaching. I hope you will participate in The Lean Professor blog (www.leanprofessor.com) so that we can learn from each other and continuously improve higher education for the benefit of students [16].

Bob Emiliani
1 June 2015
Wethersfield, Conn.

Notes

[1] Nothing in this book should be interpreted as political and nothing in this book should be used for political purposes. This is a simple story of how I have gone about improving my teaching, which others can choose to emulate.

[2] My engineering colleagues thought I was making a huge mistake by going into manufacturing. "You'll get laid off," they said. They were wrong on both counts.

[3] T. Ohno, *Toyota Production System*, Productivity Press, Portland, OR, 1988

[4] Y. Monden, *Toyota Production System*, First Edition, Engineering and Management Press, Norcross, GA, 1983

[5] See J. Krafcik, "Triumph of the Lean Production System," *Sloan Management Review*, Fall 1988, Vol. 30, No. 1, pp. 41-52 and J. Womack, D. Jones, and D. Roos, *The Machine that Changed the World*, Rawson Associates, New York, NY, 1990

[6] J. Womack and D. Jones, *Lean Thinking*, Productivity Press, New York, NY, second edition, 2003

[7] An example of critical thinking is to correct the errors in an existing batch-and-queue process. An example of supra-critical thinking is to eliminate batch-and-queue processing and replace it with flow.

[8] My engineering colleagues thought that going to purchasing was an even bigger mistake than going into manufacturing. One said: "Who did you piss off in manufacturing to end up in purchasing?" I did not piss anyone off. I wanted to learn about the business, and purchasing is an incredibly important node of business activity – one that has long had little respect but is critical to customer satisfaction and overall business success.

[9] In most colleges and universities, there continues to be institutional bias against academically qualified candidates with extensive work experience. This limits diversity among faculty, which accrediting bodies do not support. In addition, faculty with significant work experience are typically better able to impart tacit knowledge and explain and contextualize the relevancy of subject matter to students. Institutional bias reduces the quality, relevance, and value of students' educational experience – which, in part, accounts for students' and payers' diminished perception of the

value of higher education – and must be corrected by university leadership. Faculty hiring policies should be amended immediately.
[10] M.L. Emiliani, "Improving Business School Courses by Applying Lean Principles and Practices," *Quality Assurance in Education*, Vol. 12, No. 4, 2004, pp. 175-187
[11] M.L. Emiliani, "Using Kaizen to Improve Graduate Business School Degree Programs," *Quality Assurance in Education*, Vol. 13, No. 1, 2005, pp. 37-52
[12] M.L. Emiliani, "Team Leader's Kaizen Manual For Academic Courses and Programs," unpublished work, 2002 (updated 2009, 2012, and 2013).
[13] I continue to do this work despite experiencing a rapid loss of interest in Lean from RPI leadership in 2003, and no interest in Lean from my current university leadership since 2005. I do this because I want to give students the best teaching experience that I can offer at any given point in time.
[14] B. Emiliani, *Lean University: A Guide to Renewal and Prosperity*, The CLBM, LLC, 2015
[15] W. Balzer, *Lean Higher Education: Increasing the Value and Performance of University Processes*, CRC Press, Boca Raton, Fla., 2010
[16] University leaders always say that students and teaching are the most important thing. But, most faculty (and students) know that is not true. Typically, it is the budget that matters most. At the University of Rhode Island graduation ceremony on 19 May 2013, the student speaker, Matthew Hayes, noted that it was YouTube videos that got him through his business school undergraduate education. Students and teaching are the most important thing? If that were true, Matthew would have cited his teachers instead of YouTube. University administrators and faculty have to exit the bubble they have been living in. Like it or not, improving higher education for the benefit of students is in the hands of faculty. It is our duty; we cannot wait for administrators' rhetoric to match the reality.

Introduction

For decades service industry productivity has lagged manufacturing productivity. This is due in part to the long-standing view that the production of intangible services cannot be improved in the same ways that the production of tangible products can be improved. This view has changed since the early 2000s, as many professionals in service industries (including healthcare) have come to realize that their work, like manufacturing, consists of processes that can be made explicit and then significantly improved.

This is at odds with how economists view personal services. William Baumol and William Bowen described in 1966 what later became known as "Baumol's cost disease" [1]. It states that the cost of personal services rise because productivity improves at a much lower rate than inflation. Productivity may even decrease over time [2]. For constant productivity over time, higher wages increase costs unless automation can be introduced to save labor. Over time, Baumol's cost disease has become accepted wisdom. According to economist Alan Blinder [3]:

> "The problem stems from the fact that in many personal services, productivity improvements are either impossible or highly undesirable… The prediction of Baumol's disease – that the prices of personal services (such as education and entertainment) will rise... – is borne out by history. For example, the theory goes a long way toward explaining why the prices of heath care and college tuition have risen faster than the consumer price index [CPI] for decades."

Blinder characterizes productivity improvement in teaching as "highly undesirable," and therefore assumes that 100 percent of teaching is value-added and contains no waste (the terms "value-added" and "waste" are defined in Chapter 1). These assumptions are incorrect. In addition, the lack of productivity improvement in teaching does not explain why college tuition has risen faster than the consumer price index (CPI).

Overall, teaching (load credit) productivity in higher education has remained approximately constant over the last 30 years, and faculty salaries have, on average, kept pace with inflation. The cost increase comes from increases in overhead costs: administrative labor costs (high salaries), increasing numbers of administrators, reduced administrative productivity, increased infrastructure expense, and debt service [4] – most of which are costs unrelated to the personal service of faculty teaching students in classrooms.

Labor is normally divided in order to lower labor costs. Thus, higher-paid professors should not engage in administrative work that lower-paid employees could do just as well (i.e. photocopying, some grading, etc.) and likely better. But, faculty indeed perform many such activities today.

Absent a division of labor, due in part to the elimination of low-paid administrative support personnel (paradoxically, as a cost savings), university administrators remain anchored in the widespread and incorrect view that faculty productivity is the biggest problem. The answer is obvious to any highly paid administrator: have faculty teach more courses or teach more students per course. To them, it is simple arithmetic – though it completely fails to address the root cause of the problem. Unfortunately, the (incorrectly) assumed problem of low faculty productivity as the driver of higher education costs is likely to remain entrenched among university leaders and especially politicians [5].

This is where massive open online courses (MOOCs) and the like come in (hereafter referred to as "online courses"). Many university leaders and politicians see online courses as, finally, the innovative technology for the higher education service industry that provides the answer to Baumol's cost disease – despite the fact that the causation is incorrect (as attributed by Alan Blinder, for example). Online courses offer a seemingly sound economies of scale argument (e.g. one online course from Harvard can satisfy a large public university system), yet it is one that has felled many a great industrialist who processed information in ways inferior to their competitors.

Nevertheless, it is much easier for administrators to follow the online course herd and appear innovative than to actually lead efforts to improve teaching as described in this book and elsewhere [6, 7] – which is what students (customers – see Appendix I) have long asked for and are still waiting to receive. Students simply want something better than they are getting.

Online course suppliers claim to cure not only the "cost disease," but they also offer expanded student access, lower instructional and tuition costs (and hence, lower student debt), improved teaching quality, higher completion rates, and free up faculty for more classroom discussion (but which about half the students seem to have little interest participating in) – the flipped classroom. It's a miracle to those who need no evidence.

Currently, and for some time to come, online courses will represent a cost increase to colleges and universities because they must continue classroom education while at the same time fund the development, deployment (share tuition revenue with online course suppliers, and evaluation of online courses.

Online courses, in time and with appropriate oversight, will likely fill an important educational niche that will satisfy administrators, faculty, students, payers, and employers. But, online courses are not a cure-all (see Chapter 6, Notes 5 and 6), and they have the odor of a zero-sum (win-lose) solution. Faculty must thoroughly dismiss economists' view of personal services cost and productivity (though providers of other types of personal services may be less able to do so). As should administrators, but it is unclear when that will happen [8].

Professors are not prisoners of Baumol's personal service productivity problem, and students and payers are not destined to contend with ever-higher tuition prices. Faculty can learn new ways of identifying teaching problems and new methods for improving their courses. If understood and used correctly, these will improve teaching quality and increase the value proposition of higher education for students and payers.

Lower tuition and expanded access will be achieved by lowering costs through a steady reduction in university spending over time in the cost-driving budget categories (particularly as measured by growth rate since 1990, when significant deviation from CPI began). This will require the participation of faculty in kaizen, which must be led by top administrators – none of whom have been willing to do so thus far.

Low completion rates are not the sole product of limited course availability. A fishbone diagram tells us that an effect has six primary and numerous secondary, tertiary, etc., causes. Structured problem-solving should be done prior to accepting online courses as the solution for any higher education problem. At best, online courses might be an effective countermeasure for a few problems, but structured problem-solving could show that other countermeasures are more effective, or that hybrid courses (face-to-face and online) courses may be more appropriate.

The purpose of this book is to introduce the principles and practices of progressive Lean management to professors in higher education, from community colleges to top research institutions. It will help faculty understand Lean management and recognize it as a preferred means to address current and future challenges in the face-to-face mode of educational delivery to students [9] – which will still take place in most institutions.

Professors will learn that the intent of Lean management is to do no harm; that its actual intent is to develop people and improve processes in mutually beneficial ways that result in prosperity for all.

Lean is fully compatible with the successful university traditions of learning, academic freedom, and classroom autonomy, as well as professional academic traditions such as the scientific method and critical thinking. Lean is also consistent with the interests of all higher education stakeholders – including unions and their members [10]. Lean is not a means to lay people off or outsource work, nor is it a means to force higher education into a factory model or to Taylorize or corporatize higher education. If these are the outcomes, then Lean principles and methods have been thoroughly misunderstood and misapplied.

Lean principles and practices can be used by any teacher (including K-12) committed to continuously improving their work. The focus is on daily problem-solving and improving teaching in ways that do not harm key stakeholders. In fact, the requirement is better outcomes for all stakeholders, including faculty. Lean must be non-zero-sum (win-win).

Faculty members recognize that administrators' unimaginative use of worn-out routines to manage costs (budget cutting, reorganizing departments, etc.) do nothing to improve the value proposition for students. These painful, disruptive, zero-sum (win-lose) outcomes drive people apart and do not lead to the types of improvements demanded by students and other stakeholders.

Professors can either wait for administrators to discover a better way, or they can begin without them. I recommend that faculty begin without them. Students, employers, and other important stakeholders are waiting for professors to improve, so let's start now.

Let me share with you my basic way of thinking for improving teaching:

- Improved processes result in improved outcomes. If we do not understand the process, then we are guessing at ways to improve outcomes that may or may not be effective. Guessing at the causes of problems or guessing at corrective actions does not result in learning that can be effectively applied in the future.

- Don't teach students the way your teachers taught you. Lacking insight into the rationale for the method they used may lead one to repeat their teachers' mistakes. Challenge teaching traditions. Think for yourself, evaluate the appropriateness of the method, test alternatives, and determine their effectiveness. Basically, apply the plan-do-check-act (or plan-do-study-adjust) cycle to teaching. The scientific method applies to teaching as well.

- Don't piss off students. Students who are annoyed with the teacher will want to quickly forget what they were taught. In addition, it is disrespectful to piss off students and therefore inconsistent with Lean principles.

- Be responsive to student feedback. Identify the things that dissatisfy students and detract from their learning experience. Improve or eliminate these.

- Identify and eliminate waste, unevenness, and unreasonableness in academic processes (defined in Chapter 1).

- Mistake-proof all aspects of teaching. That way, students get the good grade that they want and teacher gets the learning and real-world practice outcomes that they want [11].

- Strive to achieve flow in all processes (information processed with little or no interruption).

Professors should be excellent speakers, but many are not. Good speaking is essential for good teaching. This book does not address problems related to speaking or presentation skills. If faculty are not comfortable speaking in front of people, or speak poorly, then they should seek outside help. University administration should provide extensive support for such a common need, but often they do not [12].

Like most teachers, I have a teaching philosophy:

Students must be respected, so there must not be any games, confusion, or re-work. Students' time is valuable, and so is mine.

I like to make the learning experience bilateral, meaning, that we learn from each other. I also think that learning does not have to be difficult. Instead, it should be low stress and fun. In most cases, simple is better than complex, so I try to keep things simple. This also helps to avoid common errors.

I provide information to students in small chunks because they are assimilated better than big data dumps. I do not use textbooks because they are expensive, often dated, and usually lack critical analysis – e.g. fail to present the limitations of knowledge in theory or in practice. Industry work experience should be incorporated into teaching to help transmit tacit knowledge to students. Research should be incorporated into teaching to expand explicit knowledge.

I give students several opportunities to earn grades by using many small graded assignments, rather than one or two opportunities to earn their grade. I provide feedback on graded assignments the day after they are due, while it is still fresh in students' minds.

In-class quizzes and tests waste valuable face-to-face class time and are not needed for most undergraduate and graduate courses. Fear-based learning (tests) causes stress and anxiety, which is unhealthy and reduces learning. In addition, the focus is on wrong thing: the grade versus learning important things that are useful now and in the future.

In most cases, testing crowds out useful and practical information. Some students say: "Quizzes and tests reinforce the material." Do they really? Perhaps they do for the short-term – the duration of the semester (a few weeks). However, we can see from the many corporate catastrophes that have occurred in recent years, typically led by people who tested well and received top grades, that teaching for the short-term is seriously flawed. I teach for the long-term.

I try to inspire students to develop a long-term interest in the course topic. I remind them to keep up with what is going on by reading periodicals, keep learning throughout their careers and lives, and always try to apply what they have learned to their job.

I advise students to attend class because the course will be important to their long-term interests as workers or managers, and that our personal interactions expand and improve the learning experience. I award points for attendance because attendance counts in the real (working) world. I do not award points for class participation because I do not want to penalize introverted students who prefer to learn by listening, observing, and doing the assignments. Of course, I appreciate extroverted students who like to learn, in part, by engaging in classroom discussion. Introverts appreciate that as well.

Here is what I hope to accomplish in the courses that I teach:

- Eliminate the perception that coursework is a mere "exercise" to comply with, irrelevant to the real world. Coursework should be seen by students as important to their lives or careers. The context for this and relevancy of assignments must be explained to students.

- Shift students from being test-driven to learning-driven.

- Shift students from "the professor has all the answers" to "students develop their abilities to think and find answers," and comprehend the limitations to answers.

- Improve students' abilities to acquire and process information, and to think more deeply about problems via supra-critical thinking.

- Help students become more productive persons who can apply the knowledge and competencies taught in my courses to their job.

I recommend to students that they save selected items from my courses as references material to review in the future.

Finally, formal educational experiences are truly wonderful – as far as they go. I remind students of the following:

Don't Confuse Good Grades A^+ or Obtaining a Degree with Knowing Anything.

And don't assume you're ever done learning.

I explain this by giving examples of important people in big places that failed precisely because they confused good grades with knowing something and thought they were done learning.

Before continuing, it is important to recognize that in Lean management, both process and results matter. Lean is not solely process-focused nor solely results-focused – it is both. Understanding the process in detail creates a baseline from which to continuously improve upon. Good processes yield good results, which must then be shared with others. Bad processes yield bad or inconsistent results, which must be improved (without blaming people). The improvement must be shared with others so that they can learn and improve.

In higher education administration and accreditation, the focus has recently shifted from process (means) to results (outcomes). That is a mistake. You may be told by university leaders, politicians, or accrediting bodies [13], that it is only results (outcomes) that matter, and that should be your focus. So, keep your wonderful process improvement work in the background and comply with their simple-minded requests to see outcomes.

Notes

[1] W. Baumol and W. Bowen, *Performing Arts: The Economic Dilemma*, 1966, The Twentieth Century Fund, New York, NY

[2] W. Baumol, *The Cost Disease*, Yale University Press, New Haven, Conn., 2012

[3] A. Blinder, "Offshoring: The Next Industrial Revolution?" *Foreign Affairs*, Vol. 85, No. 2, March-April 2006, p. 123

[4] See the 10-part series "The Tuition is Too Damn High" in *The Washington Post* by Dylan Matthews, beginning 26 August 2013. This existential reality is obvious to anyone upon inspection. Also, when this situation occurs, the normal, well worn, path is for management to focus cost cuts on operations (i.e. cut instructional budgets), which then further lowers the value proposition for students and payers. This is a recurring error made by managers in all industries. The work, seen by students and payers as value-creating, is viewed by administrators as the number one target for cost cutting. Instead, university leaders should comprehend and deploy the target costing methodology, which helps assure that value, cost, and price are not misaligned. This approach, coupled with quality function deployment, would make clear where online courses can be used and where they should not be used.

[5] Goodness, talk about a lack of critical thinking. Misunderstanding the actual cause of a problem is all too common and is indicative of a major teaching failure in higher education: the ability to impart critical thinking to students, some of whom later become university leaders or politicians. We must acknowledge that the level of critical thinking that professors teach to students is inadequate. Perhaps if we had done a better job teaching, the actual driver of higher education costs would be apparent to our leaders, and the use of red herrings would be seen as an instrument useful to only the uneducated.

[6] B. Emiliani, *Lean University: A Guide to Renewal and Prosperity*, The CLBM, LLC, 2015

[7] W. Balzer, *Lean Higher Education: Increasing the Value and Performance of University Processes*, CRC Press, Boca Raton, Fla., 2010

[8] Because they are usually engulfed in the thick fog of politics, where doing the right thing is nearly always compromised by illogical thinking and decision-making traps.

[9] This will translate to online learning environments as well.

[10] Union leaders have long misunderstood or ignored the Lean management system. They could be great champions and teachers if they instead gained a proper understanding of Lean management.

[11] In other words, I could care less if all of my students get As. What I care about is learning and putting learning into practice so that fewer errors are made and errors are not repeated.

[12] Remember, top administrators always say something like "students come first" or "teaching is the most important thing that we do." That cannot be the case because they typically fail to provide the resources to help faculty improve their speaking and presentation skills. Faculty mentoring and self-help are necessary but not sufficient. Administrations, faculty, and unions may finally have to take seriously proposals to create separate teaching and research tracks, in addition to the current combined track, with the ability to move between tracks over the course of one's career.

[13] Accreditation is a poor use of time and money because it drives academic programs (and institutions) to be average. Being average and accredited is inferior to being superior and unaccredited. A college or university that practiced Lean management well would have no need for accreditation. Kaizen would be occurring on a daily basis in both academic and administrative processes, in response to new ideas and changing conditions.

Something To Think About

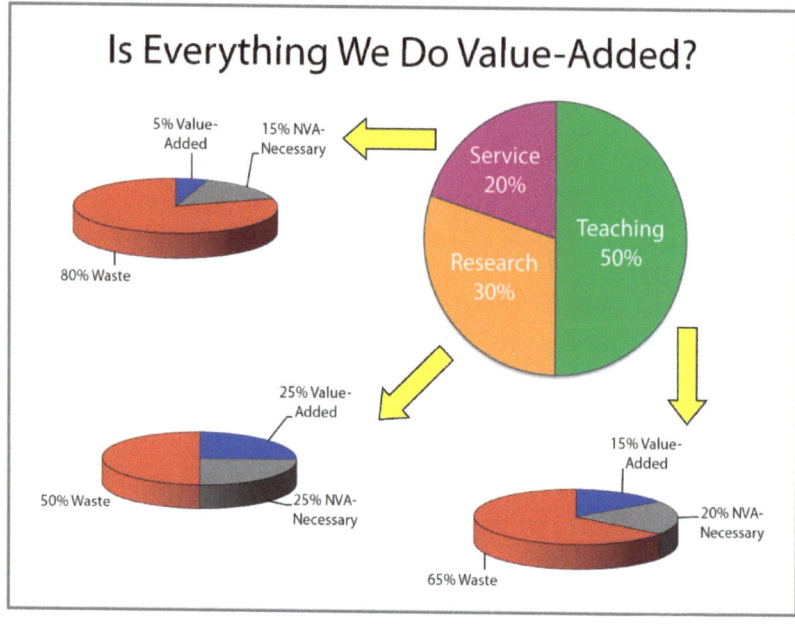

1

What Is Lean Management?

Progressive management is commonly known today as "Lean management." It is a comprehensive system of management for every part of an organization, from human resources to academics to purchasing, marketing, finance, and facilities. The management system traces its roots to the late 1800s, beginning with the work of Frederick Winslow Taylor and Frank Gilbreth. By 1910, progressive management had developed into a system called "Scientific Management." Almost from the start, there was division between Taylorists, who promoted use of the management system in its entirety, and others who promoted use of only parts of the system with the intent to drive workers harder and achieve short-term financial gains for the company.

The Scientific Management system was widely misunderstood and misapplied by managers unknown, in companies large and small. Yet, it was Taylor who got all the blame when his management system's principles and practices were fouled-up by managers and consultants. As a result, Taylor was asked to testify before Congress for three days in January 1912 to explain Scientific Management.

In defense of his management system and out of frustration for its widespread misuse, Taylor said in testimony to Congress [1]:

> "It ceases to be scientific management
> the moment it is used for bad."

All that Taylor was trying to do was to improve workplace productivity without burning people out and improve cooperation between management and workers, both in a non-zero-sum (win-win) way. These were simple but important goals for the time, yet far from the norm of how business was then conducted. Can Scientific Management be used for bad? Yes it can. But that was not Taylor's intent. It was managers who used Scientific

Management with a different intent, one that resulted in bad outcomes for people – especially employees.

Likewise, we must say exactly the same thing about Lean:

> "It ceases to be Lean management the moment it is used for bad."

Just as in Taylor's day, Lean has been used in recent times for bad. Managers apply Lean with a different intent: to speed people up, to cut costs, to lay people off, and so on. That is not the intent of Lean management [2].

Progressive management has evolved over the last 120 years and is today substantially different than it was in Taylor's day. Importantly, it has gone from various tools narrowly focused on improving production and non-production efficiency to a human-centered management system designed to be responsive to the needs of all key stakeholders [3].

Progressive Lean management is broadly focused on how to manage all aspects of an enterprise. It has been greatly improved through exceptional contributions made by managers and workers in different companies and industries. Carefully developed over time by management practitioners – not by academics – the focus of Lean management has always been on achieving practical improvements that work in the real world and that are good for people.

In recent years, organizations in a wide variety of service industries, such as healthcare, insurance, finance, state government, and, finally, higher education, have realized the opportunity that progressive Lean management represents. Understood correctly, Lean can significantly improve management practice and yield better outcomes for all key stakeholders: employees, suppliers, customers (students and payers), investors, and communities.

To do this, however, requires changes in leadership practices as well as changes in management practices. Lean management requires the leadership team of an organization to learn many new ways of thinking and doing things. Lean must be led, and to lead effectively the leaders must understand and apply Lean principles and practices daily. University leaders cannot lead an organization practicing Lean management if they do not know it themselves.

In this book, I assume university leaders have no interest in Lean management or in creating a Lean university. Instead, I assume that faculty have an interest in improving their teaching and want to use Lean principles and practices. The lack of Lean leadership is not something that faculty can control. The ability to improve one's teaching is in their control. The successful university traditions of learning, academic freedom, and classroom autonomy enable substantial improvement to occur in the absence of university leadership – from department chair to president.

This is not to give a free pass to university leaders to opt-out of Lean. They should be leading innovative and creative efforts to improve higher education, rather than adopting the same tired methods used by every other university leader. But, they don't. Instead, faculty can introduce university leaders to Lean management when opportunities arise (Note: my repeated efforts have failed at two institutions). The reality, however, is that it is more likely university leaders' buy-in may follow professors who have been successful. Only then might they be willing to learn an entirely new way of thinking and doing things.

Next, let's define Lean Management to ensure a common understanding of key terms. Without this basis of common understanding, Lean management will never prosper in an organization. Variation in people's understanding of Lean has proven to be a significant barrier in its proper application and therefore usually causes harm instead of good. When people misunderstand and misapply Lean, one or more stakeholders suffer. Therefore, it is critical to establish precise definitions, and make sincere efforts to understand and apply these definitions.

Please do not assume you understand what these definitions mean simply by reading the words. The meanings behind the definitions reveal themselves only through your own personal daily application of Lean principles and practices. This is a very important point that most people ignore.

The Lean management system is defined as [4]:

> "A non-zero-sum principle-based management system focused on creating value for end-use customers and eliminating waste, unevenness, and unreasonableness using the scientific method."

Let's have a close look at the individual parts of this definition. In non-zero-sum activities, all parties share in the gains; the so-called win-win. In contrast, zero-sum activities are when one party gains at the expense of others (win-lose). Zero-sum thinking and actions are much easier to achieve and therefore more common in organizations than non-zero-sum, despite the fact that zero-sum undercuts organizational capability-building, reduces employee involvement (teamwork), and impedes the ability of the organization to respond to changing conditions.

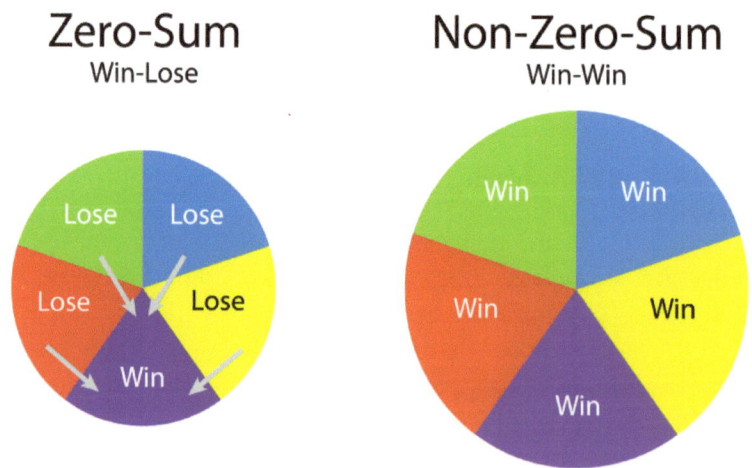

It is important to understand that non-zero-sum outcomes are rarely a perfect win-win. But, they can often be very close or exactly that. Think of it this way: While one or more stakeholders may not win as much as they would like, they do not lose as much as they could. With zero-sum outcomes, one or more stakeholders consistently tend to lose big.

Zero-sum outcomes and decisions are shortcuts, where shortcut is defined as [5]:

> "A more direct route than the customary one, or a means of saving time or effort."

Shortcuts, while often very attractive, indicate a mindset where the result matters more than the process. Shortcuts are common in conventional management practice, thus exposing the focus on results. In Lean management, both process and result matter. To get consistently good results requires processes to be understood much better than they normally are. This detailed understanding comes from daily application of the scientific method to problems.

I characterize universities as businesses in recognition of the simple fact that they offer products and services that people pay for. However, we all recognize that universities engage in other important activities to fulfill their purpose that may not fit within the scope of traditional business thinking or practice. This should not be a source of conflict because Lean management does not seek to turn all aspects of university work into business-like activities. The fit will be better in some areas than others, but no area is exempt from the need for improvement. The overriding interest is to continuously improve processes in non-zero-sum ways that are beneficial to all key stakeholders – whether they exist in administration, academics, or anywhere else.

The definition of business is [6]:

> "Commercial, industrial, or professional dealings."

University is commercial because it engages in commerce (in whole and part), industrial because higher education is an industry (production and sale of services), and professional because dedicated and educated people occupy administrative, faculty, and staff positions and deal with other professionals (current and future).

Notice that business is not formally defined as zero-sum. It is people – managers in particular – who make business zero-sum. In Lean management, we seek to ensure that business is non-zero-sum, because this is the condition that best satisfies people's basic desires. Nobody wants to be the loser.

The word "system" in the above definition of Lean management means:

> An organized and consistent set of principles and practices.

In contrast, conventional management is ad hoc and reactionary as conditions dictate.

Despite the appearance of organization and consistency, conventional management suffers greatly from disorganization and inconsistency, as well as logical inconsistencies and false assumptions. For example, the President says, "Having a Ph.D. qualifies you to teach." Yet, possessing a Ph.D. does not assure teaching abilities. This assumption is either naïve or an excuse to avoid all problems that exist in teaching and evade leadership responsibility.

The Lean management system is built on a foundation of two critical principles [7]. Both are required for its correct practice and success:

> "Continuous Improvement" and "Respect for People"

The "Continuous Improvement" principle means to improve continuously (daily), not intermittently (e.g. four times per year) or only when forced to improve (e.g. once every 50 years). Therefore, Lean practitioners are always looking for process problems (called "abnormalities") that they can improve. The more one looks, the more one finds abnormalities that can be corrected.

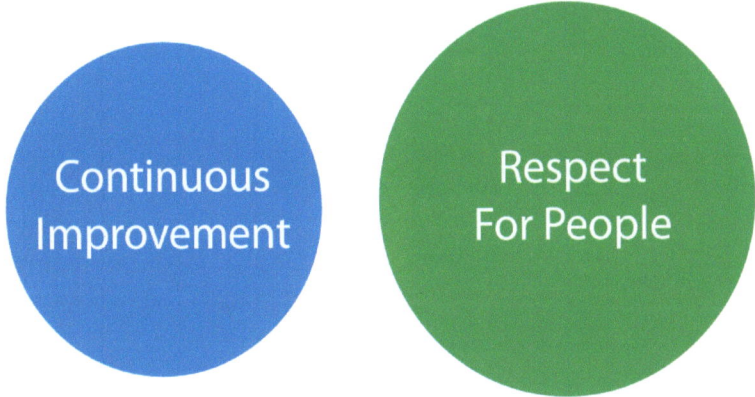

The "Respect for People" principle has been part of progressive management in one form or another almost from the beginning. Why? Because each of the pioneers of progressive management realized that people would not participate in improvement activities if they were not respected (e.g. unemployed as a result of improvement). "People" means stakeholders in the narrow context, but also humanity in the larger context.

You must clearly understand the following: "Respect for People" enables "Continuous Improvement." There is overwhelming empirical evidence that "Continuous Improvement" does not enable "Respect for People." It is common to see application of the "Continuous Improvement" principle disable the "Respect for People" principle in management's drive for short-term cost reduction. In other words, by ignoring the "Respect for People" principle, others are harmed through zero-sum outcomes. This is a fundamental error.

The term "stakeholders" identifies the five key groups of people that have long-term interests in a university's success:

> Employees, suppliers, customers,
> investors, and communities.

Universities have other important stakeholders such as alumni, foundations, employers, etc. Competitors, which all universities have, can be important stakeholders as well because they often collaborate in research, academic programs, etc.

In Lean management, particular attention is given to "end-use customers" because they are the stakeholder that defines value. Therefore, the "voice of the customer" is a very important point of focus, determined using a process called Quality Function Deployment. Generally, this refers to the person who pays for and uses the service. Sometimes, the person who uses the service is different from the person who pays for the service. In that case, the perception of value must be determined by speaking to both the user and the payer. Various things are done in Lean management to help assure that the value proposition is understood as it changes over time.

The service delivered can narrowly focus on satisfying the end-use customer's perception of value. It can also be a combination of the known features plus other features that the service provider must deliver – i.e. features that the end-use customer wants but cannot clearly articulate, or features that are required by law, policy, or outside party such as an accrediting body.

The idea is to deliver the value proposition that end-use customers desire; to get as close as possible to the actual value proposition. Doing this has the added benefit of reducing costs by eliminating what does not add value. Much can be done to improve the value proposition in higher education without compromising academic rigor. While this should always be a concern, it must never be a reason to avoid making sincere efforts to improve the value proposition on an ongoing basis. Faculty can do many simple, practical, and reasonable things to improve teaching that will greatly improve the value proposition for students and payers, as described in this book.

Most service organizations, including universities, process information using the batch-and-queue method in both academic and administrative work. Batch-and-queue is defined as:

A method of producing goods or services in which large batches of work (information) are processed that sit idle in queues for long periods of time between processing steps.

The following image depicts this situation.

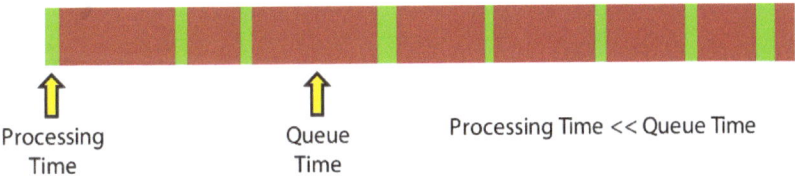

This processing method is resource intensive and results in high costs, lengthy delays, quality problems, and frequent re-work. In Lean management, we reduce batch sizes and identify and eliminate queues. Why? Because we are striving to achieve flow, which is less resource intensive and results in lower costs, fewer delays, higher quality, and less re-work. Flow, while difficult to achieve, results in better outcomes for all key stakeholders.

By understanding processes, we begin to see the myriad problems associated with batch-and-queue processing. We begin to see and understand waste, unevenness, and unreasonableness. Waste is defined as [8]:

> "Any activity that consumes resources
> but creates no value for the customer."

The resources consumed can be of any type: time, material, money, facilities, energy, labor, equipment, space, etc. Lean management recognizes eight types of waste [9, 10]:

- Defects
- Transportation
- Overproduction
- Waiting
- Processing

- Movement
- Inventory
- Behaviors

Each of these eight types of waste exist in service businesses, just as they do in any organization. The context for the eighth waste is human behaviors. Meaning, people can behave in ways that add cost but create no value. Alternatively, this can be understood as behaviors that do not add value and can be eliminated [10].

As mentioned previously, Lean management considers students (and payers) as customers. Specifically, they are end-use customers. This perspective helps provide needed focus and clarity on understanding their interests. Faculty typically determine, in isolation, what is important for students to know. As a result, they often miss opportunities to impart other relevant knowledge.

Referring to students as customers does not mean that faculty relinquish their role in determining what students need to know. Nor does it mean that any silly knowledge or information will be added to courses or programs simply because students ask for it. Nor does it mean students can ignore their responsibilities.

It means that the process for determining what students need to know becomes widened to include other perspectives, and more carefully considered in relation to factors that help shape end-use customers' perceptions of value. Improved academic rigor must be part of efforts to improve value. Customers want that, as do other stakeholders.

In Lean management, the word value means [11]:

> "The inherent worth of a product as judged by the customer and reflected in its selling price and market demand."

We recognize that people's sense of the value of an individual course or degree program is subjective, but will not let this deter us from making sincere efforts to understand and improve value from end-use customers' perspectives. This definition should not be confused with the word "value" as used in the context of financial terms such as "shareholder value," "enterprise value," "value investing," etc.

While waste is abundant in batch-and-queue processes – often as much as 90 percent of the process – unevenness and unreasonableness are often overlooked. They must not be overlooked. Unevenness is defined as [12]:

> Work activities, information, or leadership behaviors that fluctuate significantly.

Unreasonableness is defined as [13]:

> Overburdening people or equipment.

Unevenness and unreasonableness are important in Lean management because, like waste, they are also important in improving value and helping to achieve non-zero-sum outcomes. Kaizen is the principal process used to identify and eliminate waste, unevenness, and unreasonableness, and thus to improve processes. The Japanese word "kaizen" means [14]:

> "Change for the better."

The context of "change for the better" is multilateral. This is extremely important and something that most people fail to recognize. Without the multilateral context for improvement, kaizen becomes a zero-sum (win-lose) activity. Meaning, the process is improved at someone else's expense. That is not kaizen. For an improvement to qualify as an actual improvement, it must not negatively impact upstream or downstream processes or people. Nor can it negatively impact internal or external stakeholders. Kaizen must be non-zero-sum (win-win); that is a fixed requirement.

With kaizen, you learn to see things as you have never seen them, before. Supra-critical thinking makes you much smarter.

Normal Brain   Kaizen Brain

There are three principles for kaizen. They must be followed in order for kaizen to function correctly [14]:

- Process and results
- System focus
- Non-blaming, non-judgmental

Kaizen is used to make small improvements on a daily basis. It can also lead to rapid, big improvements. Kaizen is a preferred approach to improvement because infrequent, large step-function changes are much more difficult for people to achieve. One important result from kaizen is improved information flow. This occurs through large reductions in the number and duration of queues and the number of processing steps.

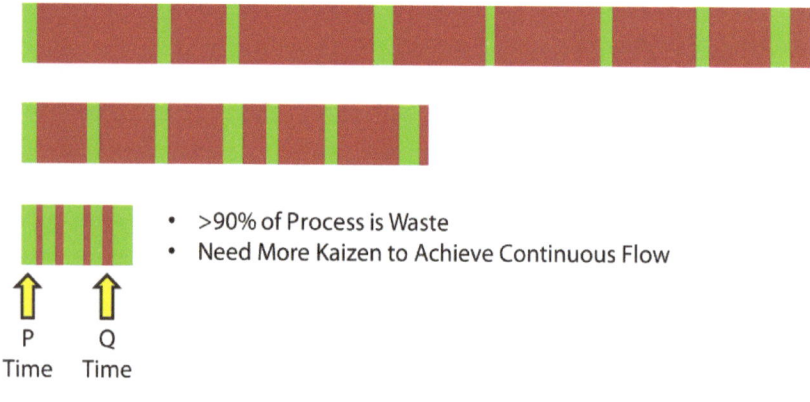

- >90% of Process is Waste
- Need More Kaizen to Achieve Continuous Flow

P Time   Q Time

The terms "buyers' markets" and "sellers' markets" helps us understand the position that universities occupy in the marketplace of higher education services available to students and payers. These terms are defined as:

> A buyers' market is a competitive marketplace where many universities (sellers) exist to satisfy customers' (buyers') wants and needs. This market favors buyers' interests.
>
> A sellers' market is a non-competitive marketplace where few universities (sellers) exist to satisfy customers' (buyers') wants and needs. This market favors sellers' interests.

Higher education is not a sellers' market, though for decades it has been managed as if it were – hence, the many problems we see today. Higher education has always been a buyers' market, and will be even more so in the future as it becomes disaggregated and globalized. Students have numerous choices to select from, even among the top-tier universities. Recognizing that students have choices removes a barrier that stands in the way of continuous improvement and of respecting people. Both administrators and faculty will be far better served by listening to the voice of the (student) customer than by ignoring it [15].

We recognize that embracing the voice of the student cannot result in a reduction in content to the point where the material becomes trivial or where course becomes too easy. Likewise, embracing the voice of the employer cannot result in an exclusive focus on a particular employer's needs. Listening to the voice of the customer should simply result in better outcomes for all stakeholders.

Various Lean tools and methods have been developed over the years to help people understand the current process condition and to identify improvement opportunities to achieve a better future state process. The tools have their origins in early 1900s industrial engineering, but were expanded and greatly improved by industrial engineers in post-World War II Japan [16, 17]. Many of the improvements in Lean tools and methods came from industrial engineers at Toyota or its affiliated companies.

Lean Management System	
A Non-Zero-Sum Principle-Based Management System Focused on Creating Value for End-Use Customers and Eliminating Waste, Unevenness, and Unreasonableness Using the Scientific Method.	
Continuous Improvement • Respect for People	Principles
Create Value for Customers / Stable Long-Term Growth — Balance / Harmony / Innovation	Key Objectives
5S	Kanban
A3 Reports	Standardized Work
Just-in-Time*	Jidoka*
Kaizen	Takt Time
Percent Loading Charts	Total Productive Maintenance
Policy Deployment	Value Stream Maps
Product-Quantity Analysis	Visual Workplace
Quality Function Deployment	Work Cells, etc.

*Toyota Production System principles

Lean tools and methods have near-universal applicability because their function is simply to help people understand and improve a process – regardless of whether it is a manufacturing or service process. They have names that are unfamiliar to most academics. A few are presented here because they will appear in Chapter 3. A more complete description of Lean tools and methods can be found elsewhere [8, 16].

The key process improvement tools or methods relevant to improving courses include:

- Five S – An abbreviation for Sort, Straighten, Shine, Standardize, Sustain. Important for establishing an organized workplace and improving quality.
- Just-in-Time – Subsequent process acquires information from the preceding process when needed, in the quantity needed, at the location needed.
- Load smoothing – Called "heijunka" in Japanese. Used to smooth fluctuations in workloads.

- Standardized work – A one-page description of the sequence of work to be performed in a process.
- Visual controls – Signs and other forms of visual information that make it easy to comprehend important information at-a-glance.

Finally, one result of the application of Lean principles and practices is that the benefits must be apparent to students and payers. The improvements must be easily recognized as beneficial to them. Therefore, the following outcomes must occur:

- Students' and payers' perception of value must increase for a constant (or higher) price through improved features and benefits.

or,

- Cost reduction must be passed on to students and payers while improving their perception of value.

There cannot be a situation, for example, where a new technology dramatically lowers the cost of instruction while tuition prices remain flat or increase. Nor can there be a situation where tuition price reduction destroys the value of educational services or of the degree. These are the wrong outcomes for students and payers (and all other stakeholders).

Notes

[1] F.W. Taylor, *Scientific Management: Comprising Shop Management, Principles of Scientific Management, Testimony Before the House Committee*, Foreword by Harlow S. Person, Harper & Brothers Publishers, New York, NY, 1947, p. 191. Note: People strongly associate Taylor's work with manufacturing. But that is not how Taylor thought of his work. In the Introduction to *The Principles of Scientific Management*, Taylor said (p. 8): "The illustrations chosen… will especially to engineers and to managers of industrial and manufacturing establishments… It is hoped, however, that it will be clear to other readers that the same principles can be applied with equal force to all social activities: to the management of our homes; the management of our farms… of our churches, our philanthropic institutions, our universities, and our governmental departments." Ignoring Taylor's work because of incorrect perceptions results in close-mindedness that can harm organizations and impair their ability to fulfill their purpose.

[2] These common mistakes are indicative of two major and widespread teaching failures in higher education: conducting research and critical thinking. It seems that most students graduate thinking that assignments requiring research were senseless academic exercises that are not useful in the real world. Once in the workforce, they misunderstand and misapply ideas, concepts, and practices, which then cause harm to others. Doing research could have helped avoid doing harm. Second, the level of critical thinking that professors teach to students is inadequate for the challenges that many of them will face as managers, whose work will have a huge impact on other people's lives and livelihoods. I use the article "For Lean Factories, No Buffer" *The Wall Street Journal* (T. Aeppel, 29 April 2011) as an example of how a systematic failure to do research by the CEO, a purchasing executive, consultants, and an economist results in bad outcomes. Many such articles can be plucked from the real world and used in class to illustrate the importance of research and supra-critical thinking post-graduation.

[3] Y. Monden, *Toyota Management System: Linking the Seven Key Functional Areas*, Productivity Press, Portland, OR, 1997

[4] B. Emiliani, *Practical Lean Leadership: A Strategic Leadership Guide for Executives*, The CLBM, LLC, Wethersfield, Conn., 2008, p. 10
[5] *The American Heritage College Dictionary*, 3rd edition, Houghton Mifflin Co., New York, 1997, p. 1261
[6] *The American Heritage College Dictionary*, 3rd edition, Houghton Mifflin Co., 1997, p. 190
[7] "The Toyota Way 2001," Toyota Motor Corporation, internal document, Toyota City, Japan, April 2001
[8] *Lean Lexicon*, 4th edition, Lean Enterprise Institute, Cambridge, MA, September 2008, p. 112
[9] T. Ohno, *Toyota Production System*, Productivity Press, Portland, OR, 1988, pp. 19-20
[10] M.L. Emiliani, "Lean Behaviors," *Management Decision*, Vol. 36, No. 9, 1998, pp. 615-631
[11] *Lean Lexicon*, 4th edition, Lean Enterprise Institute, Cambridge, MA, September 2008, p. 109
[12] Note 4, p. 13
[13] Note 4, p. 13
[14] M. Imai, "Basics of Kaizen I," Kaizen Institute of America seminar at The Hartford Graduate Center, Hartford, Conn., March 1990, p. II-3
[15] A strong argument against referring to students as customers was made by a professor in response to a recent article that appeared in *The Chronicle of Higher Education*. The professor said that in a normal transaction, the supplier has a large burden of activity, while the customer has a small burden of activity. For example, a restaurant (supplier) has a lot of work to do to fulfill a customer's dinner order, while the customer has only a little work to do. In higher education, the opposite is true. The student has a lot of work to do, while the professor (supplier) has a little work to do (sum of preparation, class time, and grading time per week). However, this assumes learning *must* be difficult and it *must* be time-consuming. To what extent do professors make it that way? Why do they do that?
[16] J. Liker, *The Toyota Way*, McGraw-Hill, New York, NY, 2004
[17] J. Shook, *Managing to Learn: Using the A3 Management Process*, Lean Enterprise Institute, Cambridge, MA, 2008

2

Unforced Teaching Errors

When we think of professionals, such as in sport or music, we think of people who make few errors. We think of people who dedicate themselves to daily practice to develop their skills and capabilities so that they make fewer and fewer errors over time. However, this does not generally seem to be the case for teaching in higher education.

Problems related to teaching can linger uncorrected for years. Such errors will annoy students and likely reduce their learning experience [1]. As professionals, teachers should seek to eliminate as many errors as they can. Consider these 45 common, unforced errors [2] made by teachers in their teaching processes:

- Cannot teach.
- Do not know the material.
- Cannot answer questions.
- Get frustrated when students ask questions.
- Cannot explain the material.
- Come to class unprepared.
- Go too fast.
- Read from the book.
- Fail to add their knowledge or perspective to a topic.
- Fail to engage class in the discussion.
- Fail to use teaching technologies.
- Style remains stagnant for 25 years.
- Do not use real-world examples.
- Frequently changes book or edition.
- Require a big expensive book, then do not use it.
- Habitually late to class.
- Class runs past end time.

- Talk about themselves or tell life stories that are irrelevant.
- Explain topic only one way.
- Tenured and don't care or give up.
- Randomly teaching different topics.
- Not communicating what students are expected to know.
- Required courses that assume extensive background or prior knowledge.
- Base final grade on just 2 or 3 exams.
- Attendance does not count as part of the grade.
- Do little more than show lots of PowerPoint slides.
- Ignore student feedback.
- Acting in vengeful ways.
- Coursework is different than syllabus.
- Give poor assignment work instructions.
- Ambiguous assignment work instructions.
- Actual grading does not reflect grading on syllabus.
- Poor feedback on projects and presentations.
- Professor acknowledges complexity of a topic or assignment but fails to explain it to students.
- Many cancelled classes (and sometimes not telling students).
- Too much PowerPoint.
- Too many videos.
- Insufficient classroom activities.
- Use of outdated teaching materials.
- Testing that is not responsive to student's individual strengths; e.g. multiple choice vs. essay (essay being the way some students would prefer to answer test questions).
- Standing in queue outside of professor's office to get help.
- Pop quizzes.
- Professors who say: "You should drop the course, but I'll still be teaching it next semester."
- Professors who say: "I'm not here to teach you. That's your job. I'm here to test you."
- Speaking to students in condescending ways.

These are not hallmarks of professionalism. Instead, they are indicative of chronic quality problems more closely correlated with amateurism.

Quality in higher education remains largely undefined. Critics of higher education often speak of the need to improve quality, yet they do not cite specific teaching errors as a source of poor quality. Instead, they generalize the existence of nebulous quality problems, usually based on standardized test scores or completion rates, and rely on accreditation as the means to assure quality or use accreditation as a proxy for good quality. You can be certain that every accredited program has many faculty who, individually or combined, make all of the 45 errors listed – and more. Accreditation does not assure quality; its principal function is to assure conformance to a curricular standard.

Based on the 45 errors, let's use this simple definition for quality in teaching:

> "Quality is the absence of known or obvious teaching errors."

Remarkably, teachers routinely carry forward traditions in teaching that pissed them off when they were students. If you did not like something when you were a student, then why would you do you do it to others as a teacher? Should you not instead think deeply about the merits of the tradition? Can it be improved? Is it even necessary?

To eliminate known or obvious errors in teaching, faculty first have to acknowledge their existence and then make improvements. In some cases, they may need to engage in a structured problem-solving process (PDCA or A3 Report) [3]. Let's examine testing, grading, and homework assignments to see where significant errors can be made.

Students like to work and learn, but most do not like tests for various reasons. That begs the question: Which courses actually need traditional, in-class tests, and which do not? After all, higher education is optional education; it is not required education. The structure and norms of K-12 education need not apply to higher education. Faculty can be creative and innovative in their efforts to ensure that learning objectives are achieved with requisite academic rigor.

The assumption is that tests and pop quizzes aid student learning and are needed to evaluate learning. The better assumption is that evaluation of student learning is needed, and testing is just one approach. In-class mid-term and final exams may be an effective way to evaluate test-taking capabilities, but is it a good way to evaluate student learning? Remember, the many corporate catastrophes that have occurred in recent years were typically led by people who tested well and received top grades.

Further, most teachers give one or two major exams per term mainly because they dislike grading. Thus, mid-term and final exams are given for the convenience of the professor, not for the benefit of students.

From the Lean perspective, mid-term and final exams represent processing of two large batches of information that have sat in queue for a long period of time. Students usually receive their graded exam weeks later, resulting in feedback that is decoupled from when the test was given. The delay renders the test result meaningless to many students because they have moved on to other things. And, of course, a test that counts for half of the grade means that students' study efforts will focus on passing the test, not on learning the material and understanding it in ways that may be relevant to their lives.

From the students' perspective, these exams are a big mistake. They do not like their grade for the course based on two exams, and the structure of the evaluation denies many students the opportunity to actually learn. Professors, focused on their perspective of teaching, evaluation, and tradition, do not see it that way.

Lean principles and practices ask people to focus on the practical and think supra-critically about processes and how to improve them (by eliminating waste, unevenness, and unreasonableness) – and accept the need to improve them again and again as things change over time. There could be some courses where mid-term and final exams make sense and achieve the desired learning outcomes. However, this would be unusual.

It is more likely, that, to achieve the desired learning outcomes for students, faculty have to do things that are less convenient for them but much better for students. For example, faculty have only 40 or so classroom hours to impart explicit as well as important tacit knowledge to students. Why waste precious class time by giving in-class tests? That means professors, instead of being idle during in-class tests, have more classroom hours available to teach during each semester [4].

A Lean professor would first determine what students must learn from the course that will help them in their personal and work lives, and enrich them as human beings. This, inclusive of inputs from the real world, would be identified as the most important material in the course. There would be an ongoing process of continuous improvement to refine what is considered most important because things change over time and with feedback. This, in turn, informs the modes of student evaluation, which will also change over time.

A Lean professor would seek to reduce the batch sizes of information given to students and reduce the number and duration of queues to enable more frequent processing of information and more timely feedback. They would think about 4 evaluations per semester, 6 evaluations per semester, and so on. Ultimately, the Lean professor would decide to give short, focused weekly assignments that are submitted the day before class, evaluated, and then discussed in class the next day [5]. Assignment question(s) would be carefully crafted to focus students' attention on the desired learning outcomes for each week and for the course, and emphasize processing the information they absorbed.

A Lean professor would also look to determine if other modes of evaluation used add unnecessary complexity to the course and cause a loss of focus among students. Are there opportunities to simplify grading while improving learning outcomes? Is the grading subjective and therefore less meaningful and potentially unfair; e.g. class participation – how do you grade introverts?

Are students put on teams simply because that is the thing to do? Do faculty put students who work full-time on teams to complete assignments, in order to teach them teamwork? Why do that when they are subject to teamwork every day at work? Will teamwork experiences in a university course deliver a meaningful real-world learning outcome for them?

Another tradition is to overwhelm students with reading material. Is all of that reading really necessary or does much of it amount to unfocused busy-work? Are lengthy term papers required because that is the tradition? Do term projects really enforce the learning or is it simply a requirement designed to keep student busy; to fill up time outside of the classroom to meet the three credit-hour requirement?

Professors are taught to think critically, and must apply that skill to their own teaching. Each one of the 45 errors represent major opportunities, that, if recognized and corrected, would be seen by students as improvements. Errors should function as a clear signal to teachers that an abnormal condition has occurred which must be corrected.

 A Teaching Error Has Occurred

An unexpected problem occurred during your teaching.

Please click OK to document and correct the error.

Time: 2/27/2014   2:21:38 PM

×

Most of these errors can be corrected by faculty individually. If successful, then, faculty must never say, "We're done." Instead, they must continue to work on problems, large and small. That is what professionals do; they continuously improve, and eventually get to the point where they can improve the fine details of their work.

A Lean professor would think about these and many more things, and would use the plan-do-check-act (PDCA) cycle every day to improve their work. Doing so will improve the value of higher education and help assure that students experience more than three or four good professors out of 40 in their undergraduate degree program.

This common outcome is indicative of a systemic lack of continuous improvement in higher education and is wholly inconsistent with the "Respect for People" principle. Together, we should strive to achieve a goal where graduating students say that 37 out of 40 of their professors were great teachers.

Notes

[1] See Preface, Note 16.

[2] Unforced errors are defined here as errors that can only be attributed to poor judgment or poor execution by a teacher. Management's tolerance for, or ignorance of, unforced teaching errors once again illustrates the point that neither students nor teaching matter most in higher education.

[3] D. Sobek and A. Smalley, *Understanding A3 Thinking: A Critical Component of Toyota's PDCA Management System*, Productivity Press, New York, NY, 2008

[4] The teacher will gain about 10 percent more teaching hours. See Chapter 1, Note 2, for ideas on what to teach during those valuable extra hours, and Note 3, above.

[5] Students prefer assignments to be "level-loaded," or smoothed throughout the semester. This concept, called heijunka in Japanese, could easily be extended to level-loading the work in all courses that students take in a given semester. Faculty would have to work together as a team, across department lines, to devise a quick and easy method by which this could be done. It would also help avoid mid-tern and end-of term peak workloads for both students and faculty.

3

Teaching Process Improvements

Soon after I joined academia full-time in 1999, I set out to apply Lean thinking to the design and delivery of my courses, beginning with a graduate course in leadership [1]. I did this for two reasons. The first was to improve consistency between the subject matter and how the course was taught. The second reason was that the correct application of Lean principles and practices normally results in higher customer (i.e. student) satisfaction. Could the same outcomes be achieved in an academic setting? Could Lean principles and practices help me become a better teacher?

The first step to assure consistency was to adopt the Lean principles "Continuous Improvement" and "Respect for People" and as many Lean practices as I could into my pedagogy. That meant that I would require myself to continuously improve every aspect of course content and delivery for as long as I teach. And it also meant that I would think and behave respectfully towards students and other stakeholders, inclusive of all manifestations [2].

Next, I thought about which parts of the course would have to be re-designed to be consistent with Lean principles and practices. The first iteration included improvement to the following:

1. Basic student stumbles
2. Framework for inquiry
3. Syllabus
4. Required reading
5. Homework assignments
6. Examinations
7. Course evaluation
8. Visual control

Each of the eight items will be reviewed in the following sequence:

- The problem.
- Waste, unevenness, or unreasonableness (WUU) generated by the problem.
- Improvement made to reduce or eliminate waste, unevenness, and unreasonableness.

1. Basic Student Stumbles

Problem: Most students, like any workers, want to do a good job. However, students often misunderstand or misinterpret course requirements and make errors. As a result of this confusion, students may not receive the grade they had hoped for an assignment or for the course.

The professor, having taught the course many times, knows exactly where students stumble but does not share that information with students. When students stumble, most professors would blame the student, saying it's their problem. But, in fact, the professor is (usually) responsible for the student's stumbles.

WUU Generated: Defects, overproduction, processing, behaviors. Unreasonableness.

Improvement: Lean professors see things differently. The improvement made was to make students aware of the common errors they make in the course. I added to the lecture notes for the first class a list of six or seven errors that lead to lower grades such as: working on the wrong assignment, not following assignment instructions, turning in late assignments, missing classes, etc. I also provided some assignment-specific guidance on errors to avoid or specific things that they should not do. These actions helped establish a more productive learning environment in which more students could succeed.

2. Framework for Inquiry

Problem: Professors typically do not explicitly discuss the fundamental basis of inquiry at the start of a course. In other words, broad guidelines for thinking about the subject matter are missing. For example, mechanical engineering courses are not normally taught with the Code of Ethics of Engineers in mind [3], except perhaps for the one course in engineering ethics. Likewise, business courses are not normally taught with the Caux Round Table *Principles for Responsible Business* in mind [4], except perhaps for the one or two courses in business ethics.

Students, therefore, must infer ethics or principles, possibly from courses taken previously, or they may simply ignore that intellectual demand or not care. Alternatively, the professor may explicitly support a single principle or sub-set of principles, without disclosing the full set of principles for students to consider. The absence of broader guidelines to focus students' thinking throughout the course, under the supervision of the teacher, means they may finish the course with erroneous views of the topic and possibly one day do harm to others – despite receiving an "A" for the course (think Wall Street, for example).

WUU Generated: Likely several of the eight wastes, depending on the harm that the student does to others in the future: defects, transportation, overproduction, waiting, processing, movement, inventory, and behaviors. Unevenness. Unreasonableness.

Improvement: Lean professors see things differently. The improvement made was to include in the course, from the outset, a code of ethics or principles from the appropriate professional society or organization to provide a deeper and more focused basis for discussion of material presented throughout the semester. The principles add context and relevancy to improve student learning outcomes and support future academic studies or productive employment. This can be further strengthened by including recent academic papers or articles from the press that illustrate the use or misuse of ethics or principles.

3. Syllabus

Problem: Professors customarily equate many pages of text with high quality or thoroughness. As a result, it is common to find course syllabi that are highly detailed and often 10 or more pages in length. Alternatively professors may simply be responding to policy set forth by the school. Either way, attempts to completely detail all aspects of the course can result in confusion among students. As in the case of contracts, more words and more pages create more opportunities for differences in interpretation of requirements, which can lead to disputes between students and professors or administrators. Confusion will also require the professor to spend a lot of time with students, clarifying matters one-on-one, and may inadvertently give inconsistent or contradictory direction to students. This can make grading more difficult or less consistent.

Lengthy syllabi may be an indication that the professor is putting far too much material in the course, possibly resulting in ambiguous or contradictory themes, which may diminish planned learning outcomes. In other words, the course may lack focus and relevance, despite good intentions. In addition, elaborate grading criteria may seem impressive but can be difficult to manage and may result in time-consuming disputes.

WUU Generated: Defects, overproduction, waiting, processing, behaviors. Unevenness. Unreasonableness.

Improvement: Lean professors see things differently. The improvement made was to focus, consolidate, simplify, and clarify course requirements in the syllabus to reduce variation in interpretation and avoid wasteful conflicts that consume time and detract from learning. Rationalizing course content and improving focus and relevance also makes it easier for the professor to stay on topic throughout the semester.

4. Required Reading

Problem: Courses typically require volumes of reading materials – books, cases, and papers, often outdated. This is likely what professors had to endure when they were students, and so it seems reasonable to them, as successful teachers, to continue the tradition. But is it? Tradition, in this case, may not be valuable to students nor effective.

It is often up to each student to sort out the relevance of the information contained in the readings for each assignment, which creates unnecessary confusion and variation. In addition, the workload that some professors impose upon students seems to assume that theirs is the only course the student is taking and that students have no other school, work, or family-related commitments. The professor is being disrespectful to students by not valuing their time. The professor is disrespectful of students in another way: by not focusing the required reading in relation to the most important student learning outcomes for the course.

WUU Generated: Transportation, overproduction, processing, movement. Unreasonableness.

Improvement: Lean professors see things differently. The improvement made was to apply a maxim used in Lean management: "less is more." This means that the manager (professor) provides focus to students so they do not to waste time and effort in the processes that they are engaged in (i.e. studying, writing, evaluation, etc.). Therefore, required readings must be focused and thematically consistent in order to achieve planned learning outcomes.

Students are assigned weekly reading that consists of peer-reviewed journal papers, periodicals, and other publications [5]. Nearly all of the material selected for reading was published recently, in order to connect the subject matter to current events and to help assure relevancy. Students read an average of about 30 pages per week. In one unique graduate course (Decision Failure Analysis), students could have up to 200 pages of focused reading in one week, two times in a semester, but they are given specific instructions on how to do the reading and key things to look for.

5. Homework Assignments

Problem: Professors give homework and students dutifully comply and complete the required assignments. Students likely think, but rarely ask the professor: "What is the objective of this assignment (or reading)?" "What is it supposed to teach us?" "How does it link to other topics?" "Why are we doing this?" Indeed, the professor may not know the answers to these questions because they may have never given it much thought. If they do not know, then how can students know? It is not reasonable for students new to a knowledge area to discern the learning objective, and it may lead to mistaken impressions or missing the point of an assignment. This can make academic work seem like a meaningless "exercise" to comply with, rather than work that could be very important to students' lives or careers.

In addition, assignments may be due every few weeks, which represents batching of information and uneven workloads. The question is, for whose convenience is the batching done: the student or professor? Further, assignments may be all individual or all team-based. If they are all individual, students may feel that they were not given opportunities to participate as a team. If assignments are all team-based, then students may feel that they did not have an opportunity to demonstrate their individual talents and capabilities.

How many pages does the professor require students to write? It is common for students to write 20 page papers three or four times per semester. What do students think about when faced with this requirement? Most will focus their attention on achieving the page count and meeting the deadline, and much less on learning – which was likely ambiguous since the learning objective of the assignment may not have been defined. Students will increase page count by importing charts, diagrams, and photos into the paper, tighten page margins, increase the font size, etc. Obviously, students are being driven to pursue an objective different than learning. In addition, plagiarism is big problem under these circumstances.

WUU Generated: Transportation, overproduction, processing, movement. Unevenness. Unreasonableness.

Improvement: Lean professors see things differently. The improvement made was to not waste students' time with respect to homework assignments because doing so annoys and distracts them. The specific improvements are: 1) Students were not left to guess the learning outcome of homework assignments. These are explicit. 2) Students were given smaller, more focused, weekly assignments to smooth the workload. 3) Careful thought was given to determine which assignments are better executed individually or by a team. 4) Require more papers, but much shorter in length (one to two pages), and higher in the quality of thinking and analysis (i.e. eliminate the filler and fluff in students' responses).

Since most professors dislike evaluating lengthy papers, why do they ask for them in the first place? Lean professors create homework assignments that ensure focused learning for students and which provide the professor with information that they can be enthusiastic about reading and learning from. Lean professors construct standard formats for assignments that can be evaluated quickly and accurately, and are returned to students in time for discussion in the next class. Short answers are normally sufficient to determine if students understood the problem, have applied critical thinking, and responded to it effectively. This approach recognizes that long papers are not needed for most assignments, but they may be useful for certain assignments.

In addition, a Lean professor will emphasize the application of the scientific method to *any* problem and require the use of formal root cause analysis methods (5 Whys or fishbone diagram) in homework assignments to develop supra-critical thinking skills. Students learn to identify the actual source of problems and identify practical countermeasures to prevent their recurrence.

Plagiarism was reduced by doing all of the following things:

- Engage students in the course by connecting its contents to their life or career.
- Provide clear learning objectives for each assignment, in writing.
- Provide specific and focused work to perform, in writing.
- Provide unambiguous instructions to perform the homework assignment, in writing.

- Tie the homework assignment to student's life or career.

6. Examinations

Problem: Exams are typically given at the mid-term and at the end of the course. In some cases, one examination is given at the end of the course, or the final examination may take the form of a semester-long project. There may also be a few additional minor grading opportunities during the semester through occasional quizzes, class participation, attendance, or team presentations. However, students typically dislike having only a few opportunities to earn grades.

Giving students just a few grading opportunities in a semester is queuing of information and then downloading large batches of information, which introduces opportunities for wasteful variation. Why give only a few substantive grading opportunities? Is it that way because that's the way it has always been done? Or, is it done primarily for the benefit the professor, to reduce their grading workload?

What about the lag time between when a mid-term or final examination is given and when students receive feedback from the professor? In most cases there is a significant delay, driven by the batch nature of examinations, the professor's schedule, or lack of interest in grading the examinations, and possibly the absence of a school policy for when assignments should be graded and returned to students (other than final examinations). While the grade is important to students, the feedback (e.g. written comments), being so delayed, may no longer be important to them because they have moved on to other matters. This diminishes learning as well as opportunities for student-teacher interaction.

WUU Generated: Defects, waiting, inventory, behaviors. Unevenness. Unreasonableness.

Improvement: Lean professors see things differently. The improvement made was to use weekly graded assignments as examinations, thereby giving students a dozen or so opportunities to earn grades. Feedback must be timely and accurate, both of which are supported by articulating the learning objective, giving weekly assignments, using standard formats for responses, and limiting the page count to one to two pages.

7. Course Evaluation

Problem: Feedback on the course and the professor are usually required by the administration and solicited from students, who remain anonymous, at the end of the semester using a survey instrument. Importantly, the professor may not receive the results of the survey in time to be used the following semester, while formal feedback obtained at the end of a course does not give the professor a chance to make changes during the course. Further, professors may ignore the feedback due to arrogance, dislike of criticism from students, or an unwillingness to change – characteristics that students with work experience find very troubling because of the requirement their employer places on them to improve their performance in response to feedback. Tenure does not exist for the purpose of ignoring student feedback.

In addition to not being timely, the survey instrument may be too long, poorly constructed, or fail to give specific and actionable feedback for improving course content and teaching effectiveness. As a result, years may pass with no significant improvement to the course.

WUU Generated: Defects, waiting, behaviors. Unevenness.

Improvement: Lean professors see things differently. The improvement made was to ask students for anonymous feedback at the mid-point of the course, in class and as a team (instructor leaves the room for 20 minutes or so). As many suggestions as possible were then incorporated into the remaining (and future) classes – and tell students which suggestions were incorporated, where, and how. This gave students the opportunity to shape the course in real time. It shows the professor is serious about improvement and that students' improvement suggestions are valued. If a suggestion cannot be acted on, then the professor tells the students why not, or gives an indication when the suggestion will be incorporated into the course.

8. Visual Control

Problem: When students successfully complete a course, they leave with lots of instructional materials: lecture notes, books, papers, assignments, etc. Most students will never return to these instructional materials, partly because it can be difficult to sort the relevant information in relation to future job-related needs. So, it sits on a bookshelf or in an attic or basement, or it goes into the garbage.

After students successfully complete a course, what will they remember about it the next day or in years to come? Will each student remember something different or nothing at all? Do students remember what the professor wanted them to remember? Did the professor even indicate specifically what he or she wanted students to remember? How can the professor know if students remembered it years later? These are unacceptable outcomes.

WUU Generated: Defects, inventory, behaviors. Unevenness. Unreasonableness.

Improvement: Lean professors see things differently. The improvement made was to summarize the entire course on a single sheet of paper. The visual control (or visual reminder) contains a combination of words and images, and uses colors to emphasize certain points or highlight common mistakes to avoid making. The professor can provide a one-page summary, or students, individually or in teams, can be challenged to create their own visual control as a final graded assignment.

Students then leave the course with a meaningful, information-rich visual control that they can display at work or at home to remind them of key teachings and what they should do with the knowledge or competencies gained.

These eight improvements resulted in the elimination of one or more of the eight wastes, unevenness, or unreasonableness. And they were done in a manner consistent with the "Respect for People" principle. Students are more satisfied with the course and the professor is more satisfied with their work having done a better job.

The next chapter examines the outcomes of these teaching process improvements. The subsequent chapter discusses additional teaching process improvements followed by a discussion of those outcomes.

Notes

[1] This chapter is based on the paper "Improving Business School Courses by Applying Lean Principles and Practices," M.L. Emiliani, *Quality Assurance in Education*, Vol. 12, No. 4, 2004, pp. 175-187

[2] Yes, that includes administrators.

[3] "Code of Ethics of Engineers," American Society of Mechanical Engineers, New York, NY, www.asme.org

[4] "Caux Round Table *Principles for Responsible Business*," Caux Round Table, Saint Paul, MN, www.cauxroundtable.org

[5] The "Real World Reading Pack" for each course contains the following statements: "NOTICE: This .pdf file must not be copied or disseminated, in whole or part, to any other person or persons, for any reason, by any means," and "FAIR USE STATEMENT: This course reading pack contains information recently collected from various sources to create a unique, practical, and timely learning experience for students. The reading pack is intended for teaching and learning; scholarly classroom discussion, commentary, and criticism; for in-class and homework assignments as part of the development of critical thinking skills, scientific analysis, reasoning, and logical thinking skills required of students in higher education; and for research, in the amount necessary to meet course and educational program objectives. This collection transforms the original works beyond their original purpose. It indexes articles into a logical sequence to facilitate teaching and student learning. The reading pack also informs students of current events and teaches the importance of reading articles daily from various news sources to stay current and to more clearly understand what has happened. Instructor recommends that students subscribe to various news sources to help assure that they stay current with events that could affect their work career, personal life, or influence future formal and informal educational decisions. The articles collected vary over time, are peculiar to the professor's interests at any given point in time, and reflect his unique industrial-academic background. Therefore, the effect on market factor is judged to be nil (zero) because the collection transforms the original works for a singular and unique purpose."

4

Outcomes Assessment

Below is a summary of how Lean principles were incorporated into the graduate course on leadership:

Continuous Improvement

- Apply the scientific method to problems.
- Use structured problem-solving processes (formal root cause analysis) to further develop supra-critical thinking skills.
- Solicit feedback from students at course mid-point to incorporate in real time.
- Respond to feedback whenever offered.

Respect for People

- Recognize that students' time is valuable to them.
- Select books, cases, and papers that are relevant, concise, and focused.
- Clearly establish both professor and student expectations.
- Clearly establish grading criteria.
- Solicit mid-term and end-of-term feedback.

Below is a summary of how Lean practices were incorporated into the graduate course on leadership.

Five S

- Course content and sequence well organized.
- Eliminate extraneous material.

Just-in-Time

- Return graded papers and projects in time for discussion in the next class.

Load Smoothing

- Workload smoothed throughout the semester using smaller weekly assignments.
- Balance of team and individual assignments.

Standardized Work

- Standard syllabus format and simple one-page schedule.
- Simplify assignments to focus students on the desired learning outcome.
- Standard format for assignments and work instructions.
- State the purpose and learning objective for each class and each assignment.

Visual Controls

- Give examples of common mistakes that students make, which reduce grades.
- Use different color paper to indicate updated or corrected course documents (or add revision number and date).
- One-page visual control (course summary).

The outcomes achieved using Lean principles and practices were successful from student perspectives, and they all contributed to improving the course. The following is a summary of the outcomes:

1. Basic Student Stumbles

Pointing out to students the common errors that they might make in taking the course and in doing assignments was successful. The number of students making such errors and the frequency of errors was greatly reduced. However, some students would not take advantage of this information and made the errors anyway.

2. Framework for Inquiry

Inclusion of a code of ethics or principles from an appropriate professional society or organization was successful. Almost without exception, students were unaware such guidelines existed. They proved to be extremely useful for establishing the fundamental basis for inquiry and guiding students' thinking about the subject matter. They also served as an anchor point to refer back to in classroom discussions and critical analysis, and some homework assignments were created that used the framework for inquiry to reinforce it importance relative to course subject matter.

3. Syllabus

The changes made to focus, shorten, and simplify the syllabus were successful. There was noticeably less confusion among students and less effort required by the instructor to correct misunderstandings. There were fewer disputes about grading and students submitted fewer incorrect assignments. However, some students would misread the syllabus and submit the wrong assignment – usually, the following week's assignment.

4. Required Reading

The "less is more" maxim worked well. Focusing the required reading, ensuring its timeliness, delivering it in smaller chunks, and making it thematically consistent to achieved planned learning outcomes was successful. However, the temptation to add material, which would reduce focus or dilute thematic consistency, was difficult to avoid. It is a challenge to add new reading material and simultaneously eliminate less interesting or outdated reading material, especially when the subject matter changes rapidly.

5. Homework Assignments

The inclusion of learning outcomes and the use of smaller, more focused weekly assignments, standard assignment formats, clearer instructions, and one to two page papers containing higher quality, short answers, proved to be very successful, as was more careful use of teams for assignments.

For students, the benefits were clearer expectations for assignments and more useful feedback. Overall, this greatly improved flow for students. However, the amount of grading per course increased dramatically. Individual assignments were submitted via e-mail as attachments, which required much more document processing. On the other hand, the time it took to grade each weekly assignment decreased significantly.

The frequency and extent of plagiarism was reduced by doing the seven things listed in Chapter 3.

6. Examinations

The use of weekly assignments, whose cumulative score reflects the final grade, proved to be very successful. It allowed the instructor to guide the students more closely, week-to-week, with respect to learning objectives and outcomes. It also allows the instructor to give much more timely and specific feedback. This also contributed to improved flow.

7. Course Evaluation

Asking students to anonymously evaluate the course at mid-term, during class and as a team, with the instructor absent, was successful. However, some students thought it quite odd and did not participate because they did not trust the instructor's intentions. Additionally, the student feedback, in the form of bullet points on a flip chart, was sometimes unclear. This required the instructor to ask clarifying questions, which runs the risk of appearing defensive or exposing the person who provided the feedback – especially if the feedback was critical of the course or professor.

To avoid these problems, the professor must be careful to ask clarifying questions in non-defensive, non-blaming, and non-judgmental ways, and students had to feel secure that the instructor would not use the feedback against them. Student fears were alleviated when they were told ahead of time that clarifying questions might be asked to better understand the nature of the feedback, but not to identify who provided the feedback.

In addition, once students saw their suggestions were incorporated into the course, they realized the professor was serious about improvement were happy to participate in the mid-term course evaluation process.

From the beginning of my teaching, I have faithfully incorporated end-of-term student course evaluation feedback into my courses.

<u>8. Visual Control</u>

Providing students a one-page summary of the most important learnings in the course was successful. Each student was given a copy at the final class, and each item on the visual control is reviewed to assure they are understood.

Here is an example of the visual control given to students in the graduate course on leadership [1].

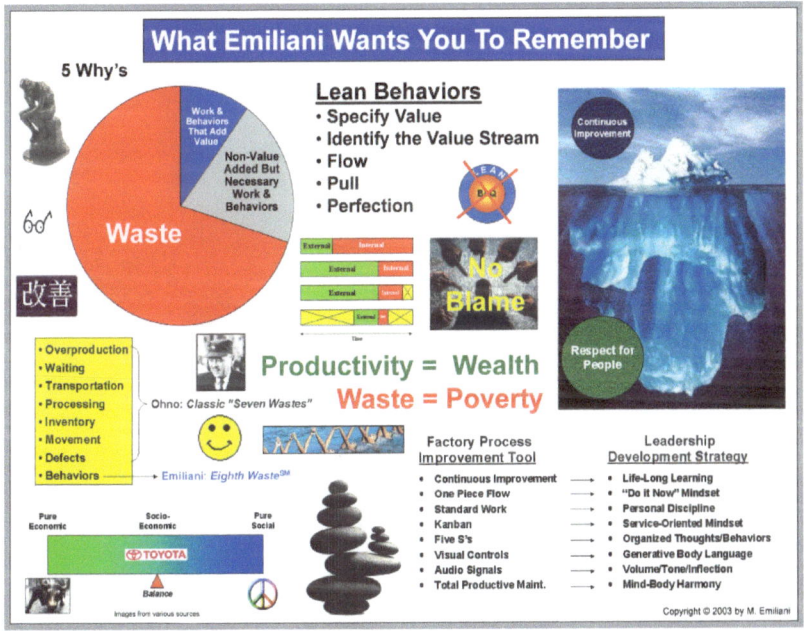

Years later, students come to me and say they still use it. Many students post the visual control on a wall in their office, and people walking by ask what it is. Former students then explain the visual control to them, thereby reinforcing what they learned years earlier. Asking students asked to create their own visual control for the course as an individual (or team assignment) gives them the task of sorting out the information contained in the course that is most important for them to remember and apply.

Students are encouraged to be creative, and are given broad latitude to create their visual control. Possible forms could include: business card size, poster, cartoon or animation, poem or song lyric, etc.

Here is an example of a unique 3-dimensional visual control created by a former student, Jennifer Peek (used with permission):

The visual controls that students submit allow the instructor to evaluate what they thought was the most valuable learning and make improvements to the course based on that feedback. However, when given as an individual (or team) assignment, the visual controls that students create seem, generally, to be less useful to them.

Most students preferred the visual control created by the professor. They apparently saw it as an important value-added part of the course.

Student Course Survey Results

The image on the following page shows the mean ratings for the graduate leadership course, starting with the introduction of the course through the fifth semester it was taught. The course ratings were determined using the IDEA (Individual Development & Educational Assessment) survey instrument, and administered as instructed by IDEA.

The ratings show improvement over time in the IDEA survey categories "Overall Excellence of Teacher" (4.7) and "Overall Excellence of Course" (4.6), resulting in top 10 percent performance in "Teaching Effectiveness" for semesters two through five. The IDEA survey of national averages for "Overall Excellence of Teacher" and "Overall Excellence of Course" were lower, 4.2 and 3.9, respectively.

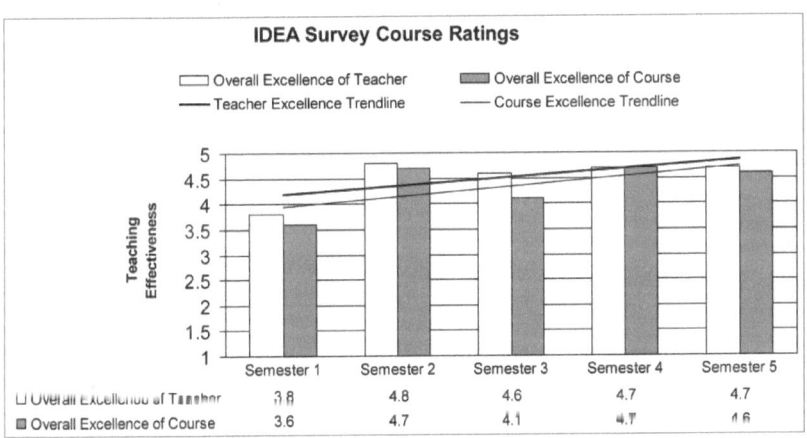

Over the same period of time, the ratings for all courses taught by all professors at my school (RPI-Hartford) were an average of 10.6 percent lower for "Overall Excellence of Teacher" and 11.8 percent lower for "Overall Excellence of Course." These results indicate that the application of Lean principles and practices to course design and delivery results in higher student satisfaction [2]. However, the IDEA survey does not evaluate creativity and innovation in teaching, and so the written comments received from students are important and reflect value as they perceive it.

Student comments (in quotes) and corresponding improvement expressed as a Lean practice (in italics), are as follows:

- "Focused material." *Five S, eliminate waste and unreasonableness.*
- "Good organization of course materials." *Five S, eliminate waste.*
- "Clear learning objectives." *Five S, eliminate waste.*
- "Standard homework format." *Standardized work, visual control, eliminate waste.*
- "Smaller assignments more frequently." *Load smoothing.*
- "Use of current papers and business press stories." *Just-in-Time.*
- "Incorporates customer wants and desires." *Voice of the customer* [3].
- "Consistent and timely feedback" *Just-in-Time, eliminate waste, unevenness, and unreasonableness.*
- "Professor 'walks the talk'." *Eliminate waste, unevenness, and unreasonableness.*
- "Concepts and tools can be applied to the workplace now." *Just-in-Time.*
- "Use of critical thinking." *Formal root cause analysis (e.g. 5 Why's).*
- "Like the one-page course summary." *Visual control, Five S, eliminate waste.*

The outcomes achieved for the graduate leadership course were successful, so I expanded these improvements to all the graduate and undergraduate courses I teach.

The following chapter discusses additional teaching process improvements followed by a discussion of those outcomes.

Notes

[1] The visual control in this example is from 2003 and was one-sided at that time. It has since evolved into a two-sided visual control, and now says at the top: "What Emiliani Wants You to Remember and Do." The images shown are from various sources (author and others).

[2] While other approaches to improvement may yield similar results, the application of Lean principles and practices to teaching clearly results in outcomes that student's value. Supra-critical (Lean) thinking about teaching is superior to plain old critical thinking. An example of plain old critical thinking is to fix problems as they occur. An example of supra-critical thinking is to determine the root cause of an error using a structured problem-solving process and identify practical countermeasures.

[3] Understanding and incorporating employers' perceptions of value in higher education is important as well. Qualitative information indicates that employers are pleased with students who have taken my courses. But, I do not know quantitatively if employers value courses that have been designed and delivered using Lean principles and practices.

5

More Teaching Process Improvements

The application of Lean principles and practices to courses soon leads professors to realize that they are on a teaching adventure. They are both explorer and scientist, discovering new ground and experimenting with new ways of doing things. It is great fun for professors who like adventure, but perhaps quite unsettling for those who don't.

I have found it a thrilling adventure that never ends [1]. I enjoy doing different experiments to improve my teaching. Experiments are carefully planned and rarely backfire, and, if they do, they are easily corrected. I am personally committed to trying new things, being responsive to feedback (from anyone), and strive to be creative and innovative in my teaching.

Each of the improvements described in Chapter 4 have evolved based upon new perspectives, new ideas, and changing circumstances. Some were abandoned, others have changed in large or small ways, and new improvements have been made. Let me bring the eight improvements up-to-date.

1. Basic Student Stumbles

Recently, I have started to think of my teaching as a giant mistake-proofing activity (poka-yoke, in the language of Lean). I am greatly troubled when students are confused, make errors in their assignments, or errors of any type (including, forgetting what they learned in the course). These are my problems, not theirs. When that happens, I immediately determine the cause and make an improvement (i.e. same day or next day). That is my daily routine.

2. Framework for Inquiry

I continue to use this in all of my courses with great success. I experiment using it in different ways as part of homework assignments.

My goal is for students to make zero errors in any aspect of the course. I want students to get the good grade that they want, but I want to be sure I get the learning and real-world practice outcomes that I want.

3. Syllabus

I am constantly making small changes and corrections to my syllabi to simplify and clarify, to reduce errors (i.e. student submits wrong assignment), confusion, and misunderstandings, and to clarify and improve course learning objectives.

For years, I had assumed that all students looked at the syllabus each week to inform them of what to do. It turns out that some students do not do that, which accounted for some of the errors they made. I recently added the image of an eye to the top left of my syllabi and emphasize to students at various points throughout the semester that they need to look at the syllabus every week.

4. Required Reading

The "less is more" maxim has worked very well. I continue to use small chunks of focused reading, thematically consistent with each week's topic, and tied to planned learning outcomes. Doing this is time-consuming, but students benefit greatly.

5. Homework Assignments

I have continued the use of smaller, more focused weekly assignments, standard assignment formats, and short answers while requiring higher quality inputs from students.

All homework assignments are individual assignments. This means a significant amount of time is spent grading per course (e.g. 25

students x 12 weekly assignments per course x 1 page = 300 pages per course per semester), while the time it takes to grade each weekly assignment is small. I recently changed how I collect and evaluate homework assignments, which I will describe later.

The only time I form teams is for in-class assignments. This eliminates problems that arise when students are asked to complete team assignments outside of the classroom.

In addition to the five items listed in Chapter 3, plagiarism was reduced doing the following:

- Make completing the homework assignment more interesting, less time-consuming, and lower risk than plagiarizing.
- Increase students' awareness of the consequences of plagiarism.

6. Examinations

I continue to use weekly assignments for all courses, whose cumulative score reflects most of the final grade. After nearly 15 years of teaching, I still do not see the need for in-class tests for any of my courses.

7. Course Evaluation

I stopped doing the mid-term anonymous course evaluations around 2004, after about three years of use. The student feedback in the first few years was extremely helpful for making numerous important course improvements. But, over time, the feedback became less helpful. Students had become largely satisfied with the course through the mid-term period. I then shifted to relying more on end-of-term student course evaluation feedback. My department's end-of-term student evaluation survey has been revised, which I will describe later.

8. Visual Control

I continue to provide students with a one-page, now two-sided, summary of the most important learnings in the course for each course I teach. The visual control (or visual reminder) is edited each semester, and periodically undergoes major revision in-step with major changes in the course. In some courses, students are given an assignment to create a course visual control.

The following page shows the visual control given to students who completed my graduate course on leadership in Spring 2013 [2]. It is printed in color and on high quality paper to convey value.

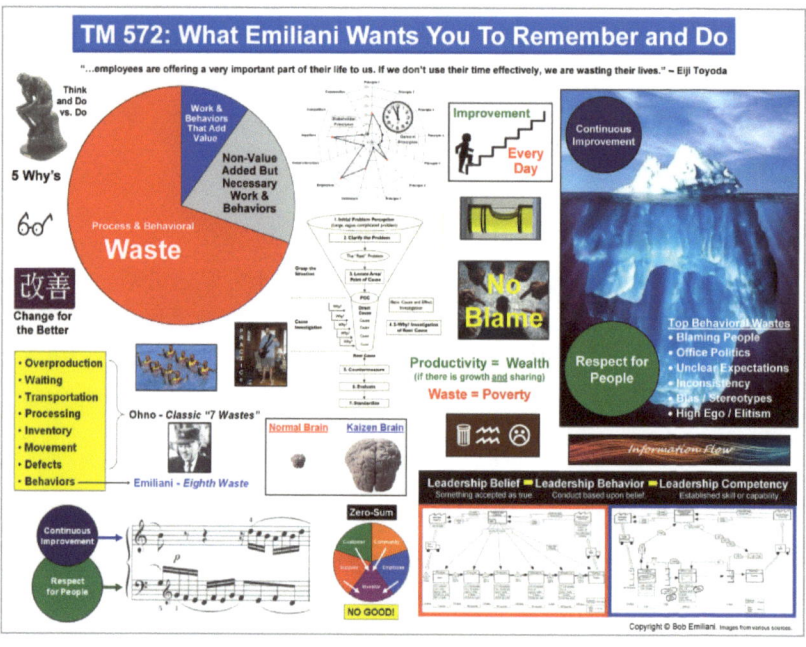

Notice the differences between the one-sided visual control shown in Chapter 4, from 2003, and the current visual control. Some items remain because they are central to the focus of the course, while other items have been added or deleted. Notice the use of color, words, images, and so on.

Page two of the visual control shows 15 leadership processes that leaders engage in (left column) and the corresponding errors leaders commonly make. The errors are shown are identified by students in a homework assignment. In this version of the visual control, leadership process errors are a prominent feature of the course and provided unabridged for students to refer to later in their careers, to avoid repeating the mistakes that their leaders make.

Recent Improvements

Learning Management System: I have not been impressed with expensive learning management systems such as Blackboard Vista, and now Blackboard Learn. Instead, I run my courses on a web site that I created www.profemiliani.net (paid for at my expense).

Prof. Bob Emiliani

Course List

TM362 • Leading Project Teams
TM562 • Supply Chain Strategy
TM572 • Innovative Leadership
TM590 • Decision Failure Analysis
TM594 • Research Methods

Course Updates (read 2x per week)
Student Course Evaluations
Contact
About

Lean Management Research (1994-Present)
Supply Chain Management Research (1996-2007)

It is a simple, password-protected web site that contains course files, lecture videos, homework assignments (Google Docs forms), and homework results. The web sites consist of a course home page, question and answer (Q&A) page (both general and course-specific), videos page (for lectures), and file upload form. It is simple, inexpensive, and easy to update.

The course home page layout is consistent with the Lean concept of visual management, where everything is in plain view and can be understood at-a-glance. It also identifies the specific knowledge that students will gain in the course and the competencies they can claim credit for if they earn a grade of B+ or better.

One of the great features is the Q&A page. Professors have to answer the same questions multiple times per course per semester, for years. It is a poor use of time and leads to inconsistent answers and errors. The Q&A page allows me to put in one location all questions and answers. I update this frequently, as new questions arise or if students are confused by my answers.

TM572 - Innovative Leadership

Course Files

Hello! This is the online course platform from which everything you need will be delivered. Click on the links below to access course files, view course videos, submit weekly homework assignments, and view consolidated homework results. My goal is to create a unique course whose subject matter you will remember and apply to your work and life for many years to come. This course is based on the premise that learning takes place when students both absorb *and* process information. In addition, the course design will enable you to recognize and correct problems that you might not otherwise recognize or know how to correct. Doing so will enhance your value at work and result in a better experience. I hope you enjoy the course! - Prof. Emiliani

You may need to refresh your browser to see the most recent links that have been added to this page (e.g. homework assignment results). Right click to save course files to your desktop. You must review the course Questions and Answers. Link to file upload form. Please do not work ahead. Use this form any time you want to give Prof. Emiliani anonymous feedback.

In TM572 you will gain the following valuable knowledge that will prepare you for further education, training, practice (self-development), or current/future employment opportunities: Lean leadership, leadership beliefs-behaviors-competencies, Lean management, behavioral waste, leadership processes, leadership process errors, standardized work for leaders, A3 reports, and visual controls. Please download and read Class 01 Four Questions.

Course Files	Videos	Homework Assignment	Homework Results PW = TM572
TM572 Syllabus Course Feedback Form	-	Reading Pack	See Question 12
Class 01 Slides	-	Class 01 HW Form	Part 1 • Part 2
Class 02 Slides	-	Class 02 HW Form	Class 02
Class 03 Slides	-	Class 03 HW Form	Class 03
Class 04 Slides	Online	Class 04 HW Form	Class 04
Class 05 Slides	-	Class 05 HW Form	Class 05
Class 06a Slides Class 06b Slides	-	Class 06 HW Form	Class 06
Class 07 Slides	-	Class 07 HW Form	Class 07
Class 08 Slides	-	Class 08 HW Form	Class 08 LPE Visual Controls
A3 Problem for Class 12	-	Class 09 HW Form	Class 09
Class 10 Slides Standard Work Results	-	Class 10 HW Form Class 10 LDVC Format	Class 10
Class 11 Slides	Online	-	-
Class 12 Slides	-	-	Class 12 A3s
Class 13 Slides	-	LDVC File Upload	-
Class 14 Slides	-	-	Visual Controls

Course files are for your personal use and must not be copied, distributed to other persons, posted on any web site, or transmitted by any means.

Students earning a grade of B+ or better in TM572 will have gained four new competencies that they can add to their resume: Leadership Effectiveness, Critical Thinking, Process Improvement, and Adaptability.

Another improvement was to eliminate sending e-mails to students to update them about the course or assignments. Often, my e-mails would not be received by some students, so they were unaware of the update. To eliminate this problem, I post course updates to a blog on my course web site. Students are advised to check the blog twice a week for updates.

Checklist: I use a checklist, shown on the following page, to organize myself before class starts. Checklists are a type of standardized work that help ensure I have everything I need for class and have identified the things that need to be discussed that day. It helps assure quality.

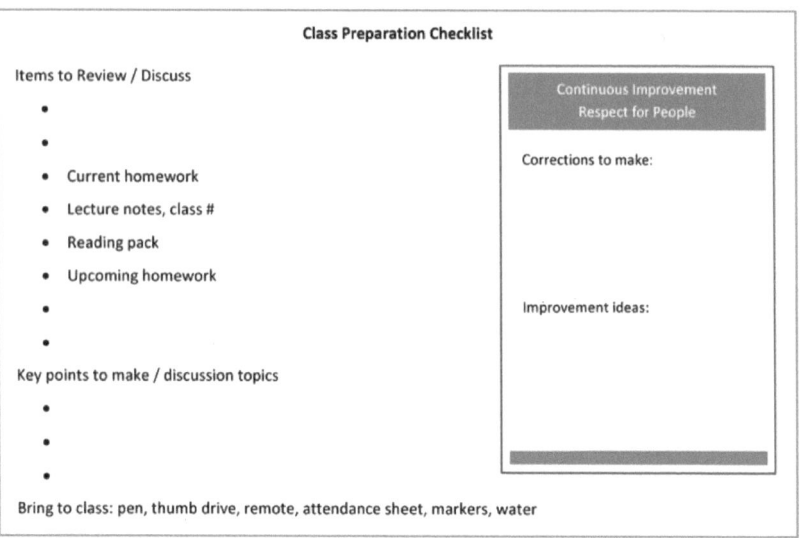

Homework Assignments: For years, students sent e-mails to me with their homework assignments attached as Microsoft Word, PowerPoint, or Excel files, or as plain e-mails (no attachment). I did it this way in part because I was dissatisfied with expensive and cumbersome learning management systems. Overall, I found them to be more labor intensive than supplying course materials offline and processing student e-mails each week.

Today, students submit most assignments online using forms I create with a Google Docs template (see next page), while other assignments are submitted using a file upload form. Upon submission, the homework forms automatically populate a row in a spreadsheet. It contains a time stamp, so I know when students submit their assignment and if they missed the deadline. I transfer this data to a formatted Excel spreadsheet. The top of the spreadsheet contains the following academic integrity statement.

TM572 - Innovative Leadership

Homework #1 Form

Back to TM572 Home Page

Please fill in the form below. I recommend you complete the assignment in MSWord and then copy-and-paste into the form below (and save all your inputs to the MSWord document). Submit homework assignments in the week that they are due - not earlier or later - and no later than 6 pm the day before class. Late assignments will not be accepted.

TM572 Homework Form

The learning objective is to understand common-sense principles for business and identify inconsistencies based on your own work experience.

CRT Principles for Business – This is an expression of non-zero-sum (win-win) principles for business. Identify where you feel your company is INCONSISTENT with the Caux Round Table Principles for Business for each of the following categories. "General Principles" (Section 2, Principles 1-7) and "Stakeholder Principles" (Section 3, Customers, Employees, Owners/Investors, etc.). Identify and explain only the inconsistencies. Leave blank if consistent.

Submit this assignment to me no later than 6 pm.
* Required

Last Name *

Student ID Number *

Week Number *

PRINCIPLE 1 – RESPECT STAKEHOLDERS BEYOND SHAREHOLDERS
Leave blank if consistent

PRINCIPLE 2 – CONTRIBUTE TO ECONOMIC, SOCIAL AND ENVIRONMENTAL DEVELOPMENT
Leave blank if consistent

PRINCIPLE 3 – BUILD TRUST BY GOING BEYOND THE LETTER OF THE LAW
Leave blank if consistent

"This homework summary is provided to you to help improve what you learn in this course and improve your overall educational experience. This .pdf file is for your personal use and must not be distributed to other students, posted on any web site, or transmitted by any other means. You must abide by CCSU's Academic Integrity Policies. Students should be aware of CCSUs Judicial Process and disciplinary procedure. By receiving this homework summary, you agree to the above conditions and requirements. Academic misconduct (cheating, plagiarism, etc.) should be immediately reported to Prof. Emiliani."

Below that is a field that contains my overall feedback on the assignment. It explains the significance of the assignment and highlights the key learnings.

I strip out each student's name, leave their student ID number, and assign the points earned for their input. The spreadsheet, with input from all the students, is converted into a secure, password-protected .pdf file, and posted on the course home page. Normally, individual homework assignments are seen only by the student and the professor. In this method, homework results are shared so that each student sees every other student's work.

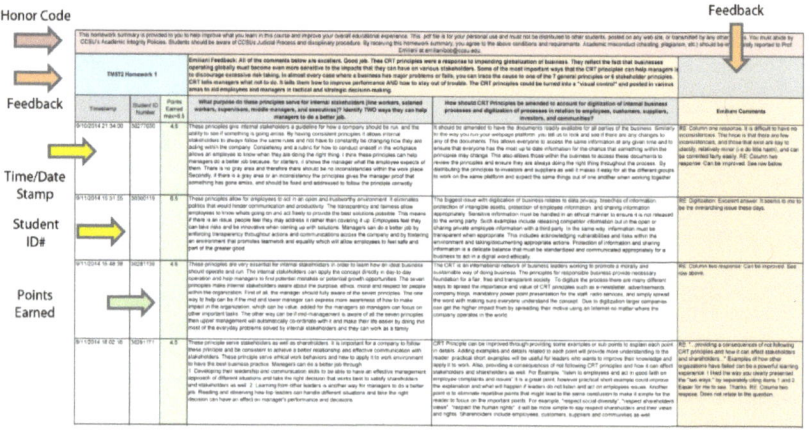

The column(s) contains students' responses to the question(s) posed in the Google Docs form. The end of each row contains an area for my feedback specific to each student's input. Individual feedback is given only to the students requiring it. Depending upon the number of students and the length of their responses, the spreadsheets are typically two to five pages long (letter size or A4).

The sharing of homework results is consistent with the Lean concept of "yokoten," which means to share information so that others can benefit. Sharing homework results may be much more beneficial to students than certain types of team-based assignments.

According to students, the benefit of doing this is that they learn from each other. They can see everyone's responses, rather than just their own. To earn more points, students improve the quality of their inputs to be more like those who scored higher. Another benefit of this method is that the professor can collect data over many semesters to analyze and improve the assignment or course, or for research. The data can also be collected over many semesters and presented to students for discussion.

Unexpectedly, plagiarism is reduced by sharing the results of all students' homework assignments. Students' homework is no longer confidential between the student and the professor. Everyone can see all inputs, and inputs that appear to have been plagiarized are called out by the professor in feedback part of the spreadsheet specific to the student's input.

This method of collecting, evaluating, and sharing homework results has limitations. For example, the more questions you ask, the wider the spreadsheet becomes which results in the need for smaller font size which makes the spreadsheet harder to read. Likewise, longer responses, require smaller font sizes which makes the spreadsheet harder to read.

Finally, Excel is limited to 1024 character per cell, so all responses must be short answers – up to about 250 words. However, short answers are nearly always sufficient to determine if the student answered the question correctly.

Standardized Formats: I have expanded the use of standardized formats, particularly in the research methods course that I teach. In the past, each research presentation looked different in almost every possible way, thus leading to inconsistency in my evaluation and greatly slowing down grading. So I provided to students a standardized research presentation format to facilitate evaluation and simplify grading. This has worked very well.

Assignment Evaluation Rubric: I use evaluation rubrics on a limited basis. I created one recently to use in the research methods course that I teach (see next page).

TM594 – Research Methods in TM and CM

Research Proposal and Research Presentation Evaluation Rubric

- Great quality work is always rewarded -

Research Element	Improvement Opportunity	Points Deducted*
Abstract 2 points	☐ Missing	-2
	☐ Unclear	-1
Problem Definition 3 points	☐ Missing	-3
	☐ Unclear	-1
Research Objective 3 points	☐ Missing	-3
	☐ Insufficient detail	-1
Research Method 4 points	☐ Missing	-4
	☐ Insufficient detail	-2
	☐ Incorrect	-1
	☐ Missing in-text citations	-5
	☐ In-text citations not in APA format	-5
Literature Review 21 points	☐ Missing	-21
	☐ Insufficient detail	-10
	☐ Padded with images and charts	-10
	☐ Missing in-text citations	-10
	☐ In-text citations not in APA format	-5
	☐ Missing citations for images	-5
	☐ Image citations not in APA format	-5
List of References 10 points	☐ Missing	-10
	☐ Not enough references	-5
	☐ Too many web references	-5
	☐ Not in APA format	-5
Other (may apply to one or more of the above categories)	☐ Spelling / grammar errors	-5
	☐ Poorly written / unclear	-15
	☐ Unattributed sources	-5
	☐ Format change / wrong headers	-5
	☐ Used wrong format	-20
	☐ Page requirement not met	-10
	☐ Turned in late	-5
	Total Debits	
	Maximum Points Available	45
	Final Score	

* You could end up with a negative score. That would be memorable.

The rubric is shared with students at the start of the semester, so that the means of evaluation will be no surprise. I fill out this form, along with a second page containing suggestions for improvement, and return it to each student with a grade. They are pleased with this method of evaluation.

The rubric has been extremely helpful for ensuring consistent evaluations, reduction of grading errors, and eliminating disputes with students.

Course Evaluation: The student course evaluation used in our department was recently revised with the intent to shorten (from 2 pages to 1 page), clarify, and provide more specific and actionable feedback to faculty for improving major course elements (see next page). It is a derivative of the student course evaluation form used previously.

MCM Department Student Course Evaluation

The purpose of this anonymous evaluation is to help improve the quality and value of higher education. Faculty will not see your responses until after final grades are issued.

Course	Section	Instructor Last Name	Date

Please think for a moment before you provide a rating for each category.

Evaluation Criteria	Rating: 1 = unacceptable, 2 = needs improvement, 3 = acceptable, 4 = above average, 5 = exceptional					
	N/A	1	2	3	4	5
Course Content						
Assigned reading helped you understand the subject.						
Homework assignments/projects helped you understand the subject.						
Tests/quizzes are fair and represent the material covered.						
Course incorporates real-world topics.						
Course objectives (listed in syllabus) was appropriate for course content.						
Course description (listed in syllabus) was accurate.						
Course Delivery						
Class met according to schedule on syllabus.						
Instructor's attitude towards students.						
Instructor was easy to reach.						
Instructor provided necessary support to complete a class requirement.						
Lab Component (If applicable)						
Instructor's ability in the lab.						
Instructor's willingness to help in the lab.						
Availability of appropriate software and hardware for lab exercise.						
Lab handouts were helpful.						
Instructor reinforced classroom content in the lab.						
Condition of the lab equipment.						
Overall Ratings						
Course						
Instructor						

Please be specific about your improvement opportunities.

Identify one or two things that would improve Course Content.
-
-

Identify one or two things that would improve Course Delivery.
-
-

Identify one or two things that would improve the Classroom, Online, or Lab experience for this course.
-
-

Identify the strongest feature and weakest characteristic of this course.
- Strongest:
- Weakest:

The student course evaluation is administered as follows:

At the start of the course, a copy of the form is given to students so that they can become familiar with the evaluation criteria. Students are asked to take notes on the form as the course progresses to use in the formal evaluation at the end of the semester.

At the end of the course and prior to leaving the room, the instructor displays the course objectives so that the students can refer to these when responding to the questions about these items. I then share with students in the current course, feedback from students from the prior semester's course. I list each "Weakness / Improvement Opportunity" in one column and then identify the "Action Taken" and explain it if necessary. This helps students understand that the professor is serious about improvement.

Feedback From Last Semester

Weakness / Improvement Opportunity	Action Taken
Maybe a couple more videos to break up the lecture.	Added a video.
Make summary for the reading pack.	No practical way to do this.
Complete A3 report in class.	OK
Cleaner PowerPoint slides (a couple were hard to digest).	None. Need to know specific slides.
Needing to type in passwords for course files.	No longer necessary.
Too many articles. Reduce the amount of reading.	Reading has been reduced and focused.
I wish there was more class participation.	Me too. Varies by semester.
Number the pages in the reading pack.	No practical way to do this (hence, weekly divider pages)
Make class earlier so I can get home in time for dinner.	None. Please contact the Provost.

Visual Controls: I have expanded the use of visual controls, with the intent of creating a memorable impression of me, the course, and the things that students learned. The following page shows an example of a two-sided card (51 x 88 mm) that I give to students at the end of the course. It's crazy, but it's fun.

Don't Forget the Crap I Taught You

It could make or break your life or your career

Bob Emiliani
emilianibob@ccsu.edu

I use the word "Crap" on the front side of the visual control card to be humorous, in the hope that it helps students remember and apply what they learned in the course. The backside of the card carries different messages depending on the course [2].

I Keep My Lean Real.

So Should You.

Know What I'm Sayin'?

I also give students a pen to remind them of the course. On the first generation pen, the words below "Prof. Bob Emiliani" read: "Don't forget the stuff I taught you." I use the word "Stuff" instead of "Crap" because a pen does not convey context as well as the larger two-sided card.

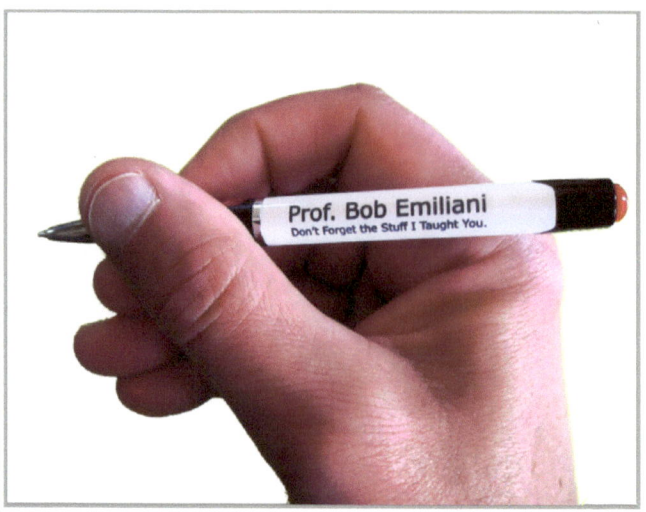

The second generation pen comes in different colors and carries a different message: "Use your education. Put it into practice."

These words challenge students more broadly in their education than just my courses. I want to see students doing the best job they can, throughout their lives, of applying what they learned from as many courses as possible: knowledge of a discipline, critical thinking, reading and numerical literacy, communication skills, intellectual curiosity, and so on.

But, I don't want them to do that because I think everything learned in university is good or beneficial. Students will never know the quality of their education if they do not put it to use. By putting what they learn into use, they will find that some of the learnings work and some don't. Some learnings work under all circumstances, some work under few or narrow circumstances, and some don't work at all. By doing this, they will learn where they need more daily practice, additional formal education, or perhaps focused training obtained just-in-time to do a particular task.

I love these visual controls (visual reminders) because they expand the innovative and creative nature of teaching. All visual controls are produced at my personal expense.

Feedback Anytime Form: Student feedback is normally given at the end of the semester. But, why wait? I added an anonymous "Feedback Anytime Form" to each course home page. Six students out of 82 made use of the form in the Fall 2013 semester. The feedback provided resulted in changes to each of the four courses taught. I will continue to use it.

The Yellow Syllabus: Every teacher assumes that students look at the syllabus to guide their work throughout the semester. By the second week of the semester, it is clear by the questions students ask that are not looking at the syllabus. What can be done to get students to look at their work instructions and avoid errors that will negatively impact their grades?

My syllabi are no more than two pages, double-sided. But, being printed on white paper means it can get lost among students' other papers. So, at the start of the semester I gave students a one-page, double-sided copy of the two pages of the syllabus that make up their work instructions.

Here is an example:

It seems that this has helped, but not to the extent that I had hoped it would.

Pull-Based Evaluation: Public university leaders, politicians, and accreditors have gone assessment crazy in recent years to answer the question:

> "What did students learn in the course or their degree program?"

It is a stupid and simplistic attempt to relate the price of higher education to the learning that has taken place. My question is different:

> "Does it make sense to assess student learning using methods that most students perform poorly on?"

It seems to me that inaccurate assessments of learning are generated if the assessment method used is one in which most students are weak.

There are many books that describe the various forms of assessment that faculty can use to evaluate classroom learning. The basic assumption is that all assessment methods, if used correctly, are good ones. What they are missing is the students' view of assessment methods.

For example: Do students like or dislike the assessment method? Does the assessment method work to students' strengths or weaknesses? Does the assessment method help the student learn the most that they can in a course? Can assessment be customized to individual students' strengths?

I want to know the answer to these questions. So, in the Fall 2013 semester, I surveyed students in the four undergraduate and graduate courses that I teach. I asked two simple questions, in relation to their undergraduate education experience (n = 79):

Question 1. What three mode(s) of learning assessment are most beneficial for you personally, to help you learn the most in a course?

Question 2. What three mode(s) of learning assessment do you hate the most?

The results, shown below, are remarkable.

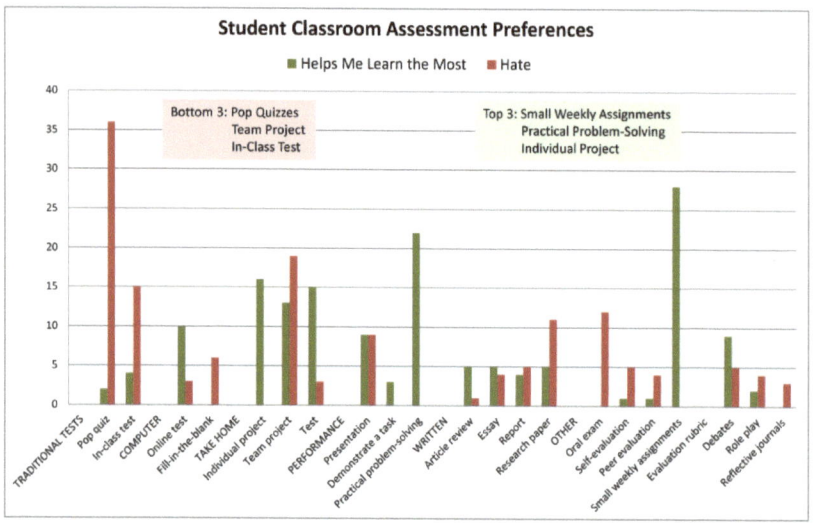

This data leads me to the following preliminary observations:
1) The bottom three assessment methods, pop quizzes, team projects, and in-class tests, are imported from K-12 into higher education. What that reveals is an indiscriminate application of assessment methods: "My teachers used XYZ assessment method on me, so I'm going to use it on my students." So much for critical thinking.

2) The continued use by professors of assessment methods that do not strongly contribute to individual students' learning experience (or greatly detract from it) constitute a repetitive error by faculty. Faculty should not make repetitive errors.

3) Some assessments methods are clearly more contributive to learning than others, for most students. This suggests assessment

methods that detract from learning should be abandoned: pop quizzes, team projects, and in-class tests. Further, pop quizzes and in-class tests consume valuable face-to-face class time that is better spent imparting tacit knowledge, while team projects perpetually suffer from free-rider problems that greatly annoy students.

4) The majority of students will learn the most they can from a course using these just three assessment methods: small weekly assignments, practical problem-solving (inclusive of structured problem-solving processes such as PDCA, formal root cause analysis, A3 reports, etc.), and individual projects.

5) Assessment can be customized to individual students' strengths; e.g. small weekly assignments or practical problem solving or individual project. Assessment for the few students who like to write could be a research paper. Or, students can pick the method(s) by which they would like to be assessed from a menu of 4 to 6 items. This would demonstrate that professor respects students (congruent with the "Respect for People" principle) and their individual learning capabilities, interests, and differences. This changes the paradigm from professors pushing their preferred form of assessment onto students, to each student pulling the method(s) of assessment that best demonstrate what they have learned. Pull systems are a fundamental feature of Lean management, and now of Lean teaching!

6) The top three assessment methods – small weekly assignments, practical problem-solving, and individual projects – are consistent with how people are taught in workplaces, especially those that correctly understand and practice Lean management. The classroom is a contrived learning environment, one that is relatively short-lived in terms of a student's life and career. The popular modes of classroom assessment – pop quizzes, team projects, and in-class tests – are widely disliked by students and also diminish learning outcomes. It also suggests that faculty are not preparing students for the workforce in terms of how learning is commonly assessed in that environment.

Obviously, higher education need not do everything the way industry does, and some types of classroom evaluation may be necessary though disliked by some students, but we should not be stupid about this. Instead, we can learn from the data and make improvements.

I plan to introduce the form below in January 2014 in an undergraduate course that will allow students to select the method(s) of classroom assessment that results in the greatest learning outcomes for them.

TM362 Student Learning Assessment Preference
One-Time Selection (no do-overs)

Instructions: Select any two methods of learning assessment. Place X in box.

Last Name	First Name	Small Weekly Assignments	Visual Control	Practical Problem-Solving	Individual Project	Take-Home Test	Team Project	Research Paper
		X	X					
		X	X					
		X	X					
		X	X					
		X	X					
		X	X					
		X	X					
		X	X					
		X	X					
		X	X					
		X	X					
		X	X					
		X	X					
		X	X					
		X	X					
		X	X					
		X	X					
		X	X					
		X	X					
		X	X					
		X	X					
		X	X					
		X	X					
		X	X					
		X	X					
Number of Assessments		N = 10		N = 2	N = 1	N = 2	N = 1	N = 1

The logic for the assessment methods selected in the table is as follows: Small weekly assignments, practical problem-solving, and individual projects are given as choices because that is what most students say they want. Individual take-home test is given as a choice because it scored highly (4th place). Team project is given as a choice because that is how people learn in the workplace. The free rider problem should be eliminated because students selecting this choice are intrinsically motivated to do a team project.

Research paper, though low scoring, is given as a choice because that is how students who love to write prefer to learn.

Note there is an "x" for every student for the small weekly assignment and visual control categories. That means every student will do small (level-loaded) weekly assignments and create a visual control describing what they learned in the course. Students like doing these two types of assignments and it results in a lot of valuable learning. Each student is free to pick one or two additional evaluation methods that they are strongest at doing and which result in the greatest learning outcomes for them.

Finally, what effect do you think pull assessment might have on enrollment, student commitment to their major, retention, time to graduation, and graduation rates [3]?

• • • • •

Lastly, I'd like to return for a moment to the Q&A page for each course and share a few things that I tell students to give you additional insights into my views. Students take the answers I provide seriously, but interpret these and other Q&A as intended – with a sense of humor. I hope you do as well.

Question: What do grades mean to you?

Answer: Not much. I structure my courses to help you focus more on learning the material than on your grade. Just because you may have received the maximum points for an assignment does not mean your work is perfect. You should always try to continuously improve your work no matter what score you receive. Also, never confuse good grades or obtaining a degree with knowing anything. And don't assume you're ever done learning. Lastly, it is better to think of letter grades as follows: A = Acceptable, B = Boring, C = Crap, D = Dreadful, F = Fuhgeddaboudit.

Question: What kind of questions piss you off?

Answer: The kinds of questions that can be easily answered by looking at the syllabus, such as: "When is _____ due?" "Do we have class on _____?" "What is the assignment?" "Where do I find the reading?" "What format should I use?"

Question: Is there anything else that pisses you off that I ought to know about?

Answer: Well, since you asked: 1) Not looking at this Q&A page. 2) Missing class or coming late to class. 3) Not following course or assignment instructions. 4) Late assignments. 5) Slacking off and then asking me for make-up assignments or extra credit. 6) Asking me if class is cancelled due to weather. 7) Asking me why I go by Bob instead of Mario (It's just a crazy nickname).

Question: What can I do to make your job easier?

Answer: Thanks for asking that question! 1) Put your name on all assignments (yes, I will take points off for no name, the quantity of which depends on how annoyed I am at that moment). 2) All assignments must be submitted on time, so that I can avoid re-processing the assignments. 3) Don't ask me when something is due; check the syllabus. 4) Closely follow all instructions on the syllabus, especially homework instructions, and online homework form instructions. 5) You can do either a great job on assignments or a crappy job on assignments - those are the easiest for me to grade. 6) I would very much appreciate it if you give me thoughtful, specific feedback on how to improve this course.

Notes

[1] Some people are put-off by an adventure that never ends. For example, many professors like to create their courses and be done. With Lean, you are never done creating your course. You are always thinking about what's wrong and how to improve. You edit lecture notes, add things, delete things, etc., almost on a daily basis. From the professor's perspective, this is time consuming and it is not fun. From the student's perspective, this is what they expect and deserve. The students' perspective is the correct one for professors to have. Additionally, professors can apply what they learn about improving their courses to improving their research work and their service work.

[2] The images shown are from various sources (author or others).

[3] Another way to improve enrollment, student commitment to their major, retention, time to graduation, and graduation rates would be to reduce batch sizes and improve both course and student throughput. For example, instead of full-time undergraduate students taking five or six courses concurrently in a 14 week semester, they would take two courses every four weeks (40 contact hours over a four week period for a 3 credit course). This format would allow students to focus more closely on the subject matter and should lead to improved learning outcomes. Faculty would teach two courses a month (September, October, November/December; January, February, March; April, May, June). Many courses could fit within format, but not all.

6

More Outcomes Assessment

The recent improvements described in Chapter 5 have been viewed favorably by students, and are consistent with what I have experienced for the last 16 years. Thoughtful application of Lean methods and tools to teaching processes, always with Lean principles squarely in mind (especially the "Respect for People" principle), result in improved outcomes. Students experience better classroom teaching, better homework assignments, and better learning outcomes. In addition, outcomes are better for the professor and appear to be better for students' employers as well [1].

Image below show my average teaching scores for the 10 years that I have been at my current university – and no cherry-picking of survey data! It shows the course and instructor ratings for all undergraduate and graduate courses that I have taught [2].. The rating scale is as follows: 1 = unacceptable; 2 = needs improvement; 3 = acceptable; 4 = above average; 5 = exceptional.

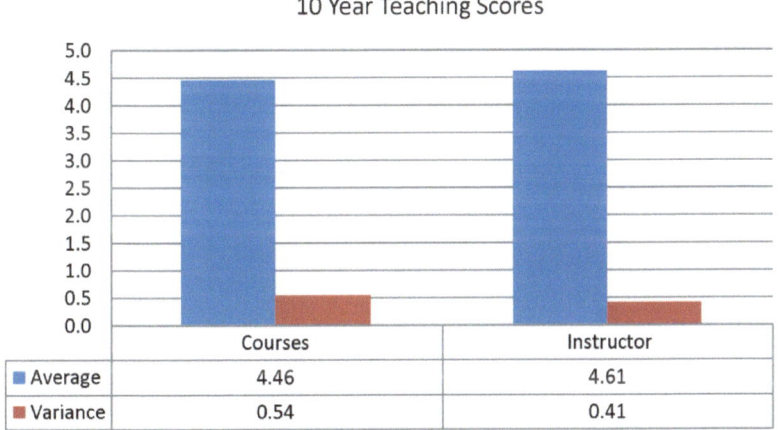

I believe that Lean teaching yields 10 to 25 percent or more increase in average scores for course and instructor, and results in greater consistency within a course and across all courses taught. The latter point is important because students often take more than one course from the same professor.

These scores are very good, but the challenge is to continuously improve. I believe that an average score of 4.7 to 4.8 is consistently achievable [3].

I would like to share comments from students about my teaching. Before doing that, let me return to what I said in the Introduction: Here is what I hope to accomplish in the courses that I teach:

- Eliminate the perception that coursework is a mere "exercise" to comply with, irrelevant to the real world. Coursework should be seen by students as important to their lives or careers.

- Shift students from being test-driven to learning-driven.

- Shift students from "the professor has all the answers" to "students develop their abilities to think and find answers" (and comprehend the limitations to answers).

- Improve students' abilities to acquire and process information, and to think more deeply about problems via supra-critical thinking.

- Help students become more productive by applying the knowledge and competencies taught in my courses to the real world.

- I recommend to students that they save selected items from my courses and review them as-needed in the future.

Here are some representative comments from students in relation to the above points (edited for clarity and brevity) [4]:

"I am happy to tell you that at my workplace I come across many situations where I am reminded of your teachings and realize they are so very important and practical."

"I really appreciate your openness during class and ability to relate to the things we experience in our careers. I wanted to thank you for the lessons and information I learned from you during my time in this program. Those lessons are things I see and use every day at work. They've help me improved how I work and how I communicate my decisions to those around me."

"Thanks for another informative and 'eye- opening' class. Oh… and the pens, those are great!"

"You gave us a handout titled 'What Emiliani Wants You To Remember.' I have found it very useful."

"Of all the classes I have taken, yours has been the one that impacted me the most! You know how cubicles are organized here, right? Well everyone has pictures. I don't have anything decorating my desk except a piece of paper with the title 'What Emiliani Wants You to Remember and Do.'"

"I learned a lot from you and I know it will only help me in the future."

"I can tell you that the leadership course of yours I took a few years ago has continued to have relevance in my work place."

"Your class taught me a lot about the mistakes that can occur in the business world. It definitely left an impression with me that will last a long time. I hung up the business card that you gave out at the last class next to my desk at work. I think that it sums up a valuable learning experience and makes me laugh every time I see it."

"Thank you for your guidance and teachings over the last year. I especially appreciated the level load of work throughout the term."

"This class is one of the most influential of my graduate studies and do hope that I can carry the lessons learned with me throughout my career."

"I found both of your courses very interesting and applicable to the real world. I found the reading, assignments, class discussions, and presentations very helpful. I have learned a lot from your lectures."

"I really enjoyed this class. It is one that I can assure you will be remembered and referenced in coming years."

"I'm sure I'll be referring to your course materials for years to come."

"I learned a lot and know you helped prepare me for my future. Thanks for always being patient and in a good mood."

"It is refreshing to learn from somebody who has 'been there, done that' in terms of the course material."

"I found this class very beneficial. I can honestly say it will have an impact on how I manage my activities and deal with people on a personal and professional level."

"Let me express how much I appreciated this course. You have created something very interesting, enjoyable, compelling, and definitely leading edge."

"In my honest opinion, your leadership course was one of the three most valuable classes for me."

"This class has been one of the most practical and beneficial of all the classes I've taken in the Master's program."

"I plan to keep the materials from class for reference."

"I enjoyed your class very much and it has helped me a lot in my own work outside of school."

"I wanted to thank you and let you know how much I enjoyed your classes. I highly recommend them to people that I work with. I appreciate all that you and the other faculty members have done to improve the program and make it a more enjoyable experience for the students."

"I just wanted to tell you how much I enjoyed your class and your teaching style. I feel that I really learned a lot and in fact have already applied some of the things that I have learned in class to my everyday life at my job. Your teaching was very unique, the way that you spoke 'to' the class and not 'at' the class. Not having tests was also something that was completely different than other classes. When you first handed out the syllabus I thought that the class was going to be a joke and extremely easy. The truth is, not having tests actually helped me to pay attention more and learn more because it seemed like instead of cramming for a test like I do in most of my classes my attention was instead focused on the class discussions and the information that I feel will help me most in my business career. Overall the class was a great learning experience."

"Not too long ago another fellow and myself from the program were commenting on the relevant information that we learned from your class, and both had come to the conclusion that you were one of the best teachers at CCSU."

"The subject matter you selected had a real impact and will stay with me for a while."

• • • • •

The improvements were readily apparent to students and easily recognized as beneficial to their interests. The benefits of my application of Lean principles and practices were apparent to students in the form of higher value (constant price but with improved features). That outcome was within my control and I achieved it.

More important than the score for the course and score for the instructor is the fact than most students seem to learn the material, remember what they learned, *and* apply what they learned. That makes me very happy.

In the future, I expect that the expanded use of teaching technologies (learning management systems, online courses, etc.), will require teachers to think more along the lines of what has been presented in this book. Increased use of technology does not eliminate the need for Lean thinking; it increases the need for Lean thinking because technology is significant process change [5, 6], and, like many process changes, may not be driven by actual student needs and it may not improve flow. Lean principles and practices will remain useful as means to improve teaching as higher education evolves [6].

Recall what I said In the Introduction: "Online courses offer a seemingly sound economies of scale argument, yet it is one that has felled many a great industrialist who processed information in ways inferior to their competitors."

The way forward is to process information, in both academic and administrative processes, much better than the universities that embrace expensive technologies (e.g. online curses) as the solution to Baumol's cost disease. In other words, colleges and universities that use Lean principles and practices to rapidly eliminate waste, unevenness, and unreasonableness, will reduce costs and greatly improve the value proposition for students. This could reduce the attractiveness of technology for use in higher education, at least among those students who prefer face-to-face or hybrid courses.

The challenge for top university administrators, staff, and faculty is to correctly understand and practice Lean management, and, working together, transform higher education to deliver to students a great educational experience and the value that they expect to receive. That should be the goal.

New technologies do not place that demand on higher education personnel. Instead, they avoid it. Therefore, they likely will not improve the value proposition for students and payers. In addition, online courses, while presently offed as non-zero-sum, could become zero-sum if colleges and universities do not quickly achieve the expected cost savings or other purported benefits [7].

Notes

[1] This statement is based on conversations with hiring managers. Quantitative data supporting this statement is lacking at this time.

[2] The survey instrument is comprised of 24 questions. The data presented are based on questions 16 ("Rate overall quality / satisfaction of course") and 17 ("Rate overall quality of instruction"). This survey has been replaced by the one shown in Chapter 5. The current course ratings are lower than the IDEA Center survey shown in Chapter 4 because it is an average of six different courses (i.e. distinctly different topics) versus one course for the IDEA survey.

[3] Higher scores are not likely because some students do not have interest in the
subject matter contained in the course, while others dislike flow and prefer the batch-and-queue teaching that they have experienced for so many years. They have grown to like pop quizzes, mid-term and final exams, ambiguous assignments, condescending professors, and the like. To them, pain is synonymous with learning. I accommodate those few students by including in my syllabi the following: "These are minimum course requirements. If you feel you would get more out of this course through tests, projects, term papers, etc., please let me know." I have had no takers.

[4] Obviously, not all student comments are like these (See Note 3). However, they accurately portray the general sentiment of a great majority (~90 percent) of students towards how I teach.

[5] I do not take as axiomatic that online courses lower instructional costs, either on a unit cost basis or a total cost basis. Online courses and degree programs will create many new costs for a university (e.g. new support services, advertising, assessment, lawsuits) or for students (e.g. under-employment or low pay) that could make traditional classroom education look inexpensive and far more valuable. Nor do I take as axiomatic that online courses increase revenue because they may not turn out to be a better product. New does not mean better. Hence, the continued need for Lean thinking, for both old and new processes.

[6] And it is especially useful for imparting supra-critical (Lean) thinking to students. For example, anyone offering a nearly all

upside and no downside cure for a problem should automatically trigger intense supra-critical thinking and thorough due diligence by affected stakeholders. If interest in online courses continues, then here are some questions the institution should ask of itself and of online course suppliers:

- What is the root cause of the problem(s) that online courses correct? Show me your problem-solving analyses.
- What is the reduction in unit instructional costs using online courses? Show me exactly how unit cost reductions are achieved, and how the savings accrue over time.
- What is the reduction in total costs that a college or university can expect? Show us exactly how total costs decline as a function of time.
- Which university departments will experience higher recurring operating costs?
- What cost increases can the following stakeholders expect: students, payers, employers, and taxpayers?
- Why should I believe your savings estimates when estimates and forecasts are wrong more than 30 percent of the time?
- What specific teaching quality problems do online courses correct? How do they affect student engagement, learning outcomes, completion, and post-graduation success?
- What specific teaching quality problems do online courses create? How do they affect student engagement, learning outcomes, completion, and post-graduation success?
- Will completion of lower-level courses by greater numbers of students via online courses create course availability problems when students enter their major areas of study in years 3 and 4? Will online courses be the answer for that too?
- What criteria do you use to determine a online professor's professor's teaching effectiveness?
- How do online courses help us achieve our institution's future state goal of delivering more value to students at the same or lower prices?
- Do online courses preserve the "sage on stage" current state?
- How do you measure quality and reduce course-to-course variation? What system do you use to assure quality?

- Will online courses increase or decrease our flexibility to make rapid or frequent adjustments or improvements? What is the time and cost associated with editing or eliminating online courses as curriculum committees make changes?
- What is the process for improving online courses that have already been created? Can they be updated weekly or monthly? What is the time and cost associated with frequently updating or adding new information to online courses as subject area knowledge or pedagogy change.
- How long is the useful life of online courses in the rapidly changing information age?

University leaders and politicians would be wise to seek information that contradicts online course suppliers' claims, lest they fall victim to confirmation bias and other decision-making traps and accidentally increase total cost in their rush to reduce unit costs, expand access, or increase completion rates. As educated persons, University leaders and politicians should make sincere efforts to ensure they do not suffer from illogical thinking and proffer fatuous arguments for major process changes. A not-so-wise Provost offered this argument for online courses: "...you can't ignore the sea change – you can only embrace it..." You can ignore it if you think. The unintended consequences could be many and varied: strengthening of shared governance; higher faculty pay; higher administrative costs; vacancies in on-campus housing; declining revenues from food services; cheating scandals; reduction in brand equity; fewer classroom courses or sections; faculty exit academia; new PhDs shun academia; labor disputes; decline in research funding; reduction in income-generating intellectual property assets; reduction in tuition income; reduction in alumni giving; decline in sales of branded merchandise; reduction in state and federal appropriations; increased endowment investment risk to achieve higher returns; increased outsourcing; non-profit tax status challenges; accreditation problems and conflicts; problems with state and federal HE regulators; decline in the value of higher education as perceived by students, payers, and employers (value = function/cost); lower enrollments; high administrative turnover; increased costs associated with recruiting new administrators; costly and time-consuming defensive routines that make full use of illogical thinking and decision-making traps; and so on. To accept the upsides of new technologies in higher education and diminish or ignore potential downsides (and forego contingencies) is a hallmark of poor institutional leadership.

[7] Many university administrators will be forced to reap labor savings through a reduction in full-time faculty, cut the pay to those who lead classroom discussions, reduce the influence of unions, or similar zero-sum outcomes. Others will be unable to resist the temptation to take these or other zero-sum actions.

7

Closing Remarks

I wrote this book to share with faculty the creative and innovative ways that I have gone about improving my teaching. It is based the supra-critical (Lean) thinking that I learned in the manufacturing industry and adapted to the higher education service industry.

The image below illustrates the problem that Lean principles and practices helped me address when I first began teaching full-time in 1999.

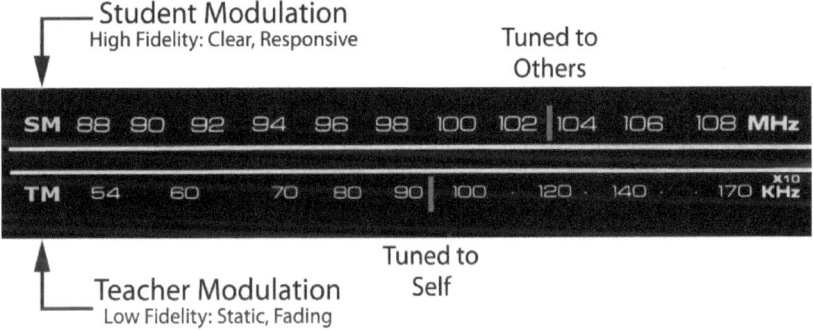

Namely, tuning into student feedback, as opposed to largely ignoring that feedback and doing what I thought was best for students – from my own narrow perspective and whose basic training in teaching consisted of doing what my teachers did. I knew that was not the right approach and that I could do better.
Professors must realize that being stuck on "Teacher Modulation" means that improvement occurs much more slowly than is needed by students, payers, and employers – even for small improvements. Teachers and administrators must instead be tuned to "Student Modulation" to keep up with the times and assure relevancy as conditions change.

The image on the following page shows actual time in hours, minutes, and seconds, while university time is in months, weeks, and days. The large gap between the two is not acceptable. The gap must be narrowed to reflect the reality of the higher education buyers' market and its customers' needs.

For too many years students have endured undergraduate or graduate studies in which 10 percent of the professors were above average to exceptional, while the remaining 90 percent were acceptable to awful. We should not be surprised that students and payers would one day question the value of such an experience given its cost, and the desire for outcomes that meet or exceed expectations. My intense focus on "Student Modulation" has resulted in outcomes better aligned with students' desires while still achieving the learning objectives I strive to deliver.

But, the larger problem remains: One out of 10 professors is above average to exceptional. That has to be flipped around – which is a far more critical needed than flipping classrooms around. The causes of the "10 percent problem" must be found and corrected.

Faculty can surrender and allow new technology to deliver the most of teaching and some of the learning, or they can instead do many simple yet highly effective things to improve both their teaching and students' learning experience. To succeed, many more professors need to become "Student Modulated." I am confident that our teaching can and must be far more effective than online courses – video courses that could be viewed by students as a mere "exercise" to comply with, irrelevant to the real world [1]. We can do better than that.

Any professor can do what I have done, which I think, has simply been to more closely align learning inside of school with how people normally learn outside of school. Fundamentally, it is students learning from teachers, live, through small practical lessons, continuously, in a natural environment versus large abstract lessons, periodically, in a contrived environment. This might not make much sense to those who easily excel in school, but it probably makes a lot of sense to those who do not.

And, this was done at lower cost and with far greater flexibility than expensive learning management systems or elaborate online courses, with no unfavorable outcomes or costly unintended consequences. In other words, it is a simple way to improve that works. Applying Lean principles and practices to teaching is a series of many small process changes. In contrast, new technologies are large step-function changes that will be far more challenging to implement than anyone expects, with results, that, over time, could disappoint [2].

The successful outcomes that I have achieved are partly the result of the knowledge of Lean management that I acquired through 20 years of practice in industry, self-study, and research. Professors interested in doing what I have done should take it upon themselves to learn more about Lean management. Learn as much as you can, as fast as you can, by putting into practice what you read here and elsewhere.

I have provided some key readings in Notes [3] to [9]. These should be very helpful for learning Lean principles and practices. You will also begin to learn the basic way of thinking, which includes the non-zero-sum mindset required by the "Respect for People" principle. Do not underestimate the degree to which the thinking is different. If you do, then you will fail to comprehend the nuances and details that help deliver successful outcomes.

Reading is good, but Lean is learned by doing. You will learn though a lot of trial-and-error. Fortunately, mistakes tend to be small and easily corrected. I urge you to experiment and try new things. Don't be afraid to fail. Don't try something, say "it did not work," and then give up. Lean people ask, "Why did it fail?" They seek to understand the cause of failure and try again – and again and again. They are tenacious problems-solvers because improvement is important to all stakeholders – especially, in our context of students, payers, employers, and society.

Many people, especially leaders, make the mistake of turning improvement into unpleasant chore. Improvement – Lean teaching – must be fun, otherwise people will avoid it. I have a lot of fun doing what I have described in this book [10]. I am sure you will too.

You can take your individual effort to improve your teaching one step further by applying the kaizen process to improve academic programs [11-14]. This team-based activity accelerates improvement across the institution and generates new and valuable interactions between faculty, staff, students, alumni, and employers.

You will benefit greatly by participating in kaizens that take place in companies or organizations in your town, whether manufacturing or service. Generally, manufacturing kaizens are more impactful and therefore result in a better learning experience, which you can then translate to your teaching environment. Note that the kaizen experience depends a lot on the kaizen facilitator and management's understanding of kaizen. There is such a thing as bad kaizen. If you happen to experience this, please do not assume all kaizens are that way. To the extent possible, try to participate in kaizens in organizations that understand kaizen and have good facilitators [15].

Learning to think differently and do things differently is big a challenge. In Lean, we use visual controls to remind is of what we must do or how to think about problems. The following two pages show my "Lean Educator's Visual Control." Most of the items are

Closing Remarks   103

self-explanatory. You can download a copy from my web site, www.leanprofessor.com. Use it every day to help improve your teaching.

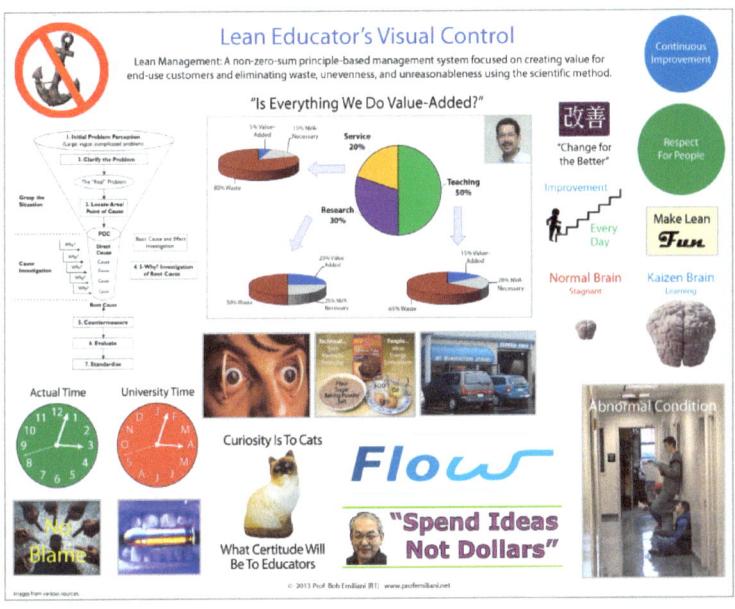

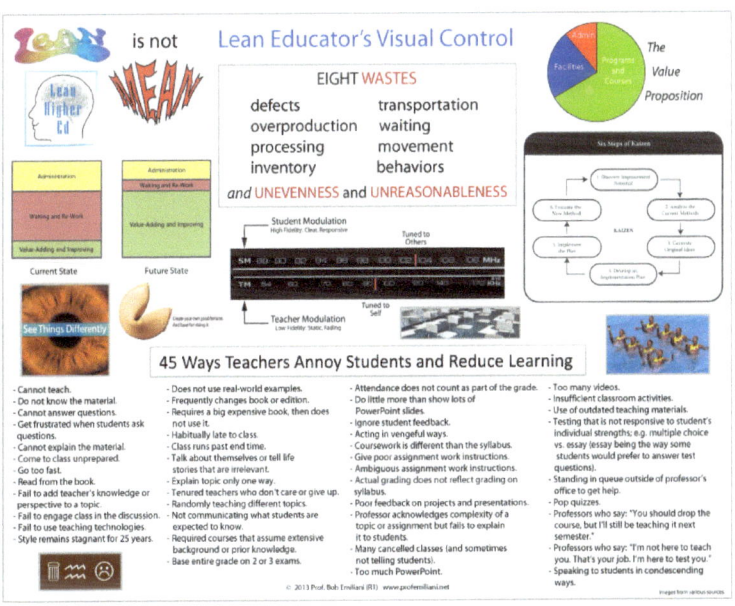

I hope you have found this book informative and inspirational. To learn more about kaizen, please read this important book:

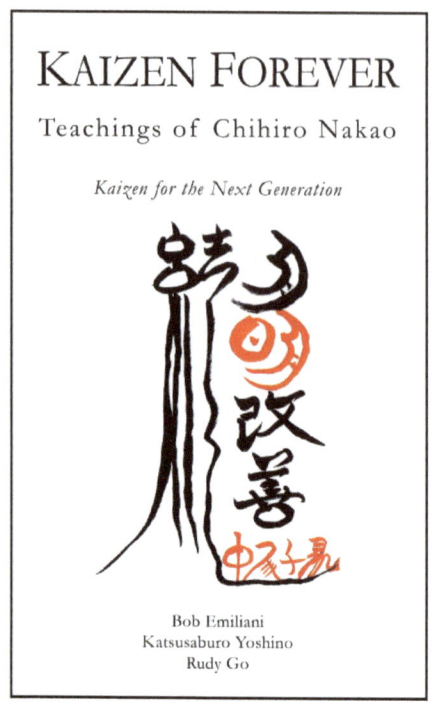

And, please participate in The Lean Professor blog so we can continue the conversation!

Together we learn and improve.

Notes

[1] Due in part to poor course design or faculty who may lack industry work experience, which could limit the ability to impart tacit knowledge, explain and contextualize the relevancy of subject matter to students, or demonstrate the practical limits of knowledge.

[2] I recognize the benefits of online content, particularly when used in a hybrid format. Presently, the main advantages of online courses from students' perspective include: Control the learning experience (learn exactly what I want); complete assignments on own time; course feels simplified/streamlined to what you really need to know; play or replay lectures at your leisure; can pace your own learning; less pressure (not put on the spot as in a classroom); don't have a constricting or dull classroom setting; online materials help you stay organized and avoid losing important papers; no group work; no arbitrary (professors') standards of excellence; not having to work with difficult professors. Disadvantages for students include: Feel distant from the professor; more difficult to get extra help (and possibly reduced learning); lose spontaneous classroom discussion or debate; not hearing professor explain something or hearing the way they talk about certain subjects (reduces understanding); no social interaction; distractions (browse the Internet). To my ears, this translates as: "I want to learn and I am willing to work, but please make learning easier and more convenient. Stop doing things that turn us off and make it more of a pleasure to interact with you (the teacher)." As this book has shown, new technologies are not needed to deliver to students the learning experience that they seek.

[3] B. Emiliani et al., *Better Thinking, Better Results*, The CLBM, LLC, Wethersfield, Conn., second edition, 2007

[4] C. Kenney, *Transforming Health Care: Virginia Mason Medical Center's Pursuit of the Perfect Patient Experience*, CRC Press, Boca Raton, FL, 2011

[5] A. Byrne, *The Lean Turnaround*, McGraw-Hill, New York, NY, 2012

[6] J. Womack and D. Jones, *Lean Thinking*, Productivity Press, New York, NY, second edition, 2003

[7] J. Liker, *The Toyota Way*, McGraw-Hill, New York, NY, 2004

[8] N. Modig and P. Åhlström, *This Is Lean*, Rheologica Publishing, Stockholm, Sweden, 2012

[9] T. Ohno, *Toyota Production System*, Productivity Press, Portland, OR, 1988

[10] For example, one thing I have fun with is "red tagging," which means to separate needed items from those that are not needed. It's a fun challenge to figure out items not needed and "red tag" them for disposal, such as textbooks, expensive learning management systems, lengthy term papers, etc. Doing so supports Five S, specifically, *sort*, which helps create a more organized teaching workspace and improve quality.

[11] M.L. Emiliani, "Using Kaizen to Improve Graduate Business School Degree Programs," *Quality Assurance in Education*, Vol. 13, No. 1, 2005, pp. 37-52

[12] M.L. Emiliani, "Team Leader's Kaizen Manual For Academic Courses and Programs," unpublished work, 2002 (updated 2009 and 2012).

[13] I. Kato and A. Smalley, *Toyota Kaizen Methods*, CRC Press, Boca Raton, FL, 2011

[14] M. Imai, *Gemba Kaizen*, second edition, McGraw-Hill, New York, NY, 2012

[15] One of my kaizen teachers, Doi Yoshihisa, taught me that it is not sufficient to have a kaizen mind, but one must also have a kaizen heart to assure that kaizen does not harm people. Progressive Lean management is a human-centered management system, and so kaizen, a fundamental process for learning Lean management, must be a balance of both heart and mind.

Appendix I

Imaginary Customers

Most professors and many administrators have great difficulty accepting the idea of students as customers. Some put great effort into finding ways to describe students as anything but customers. They are partners, they are empowered learners, they are producers, and so on.

The resistance to accept students as customers is perhaps because most people do not like to serve others, even though it may be their job to do so. In truth, we would rather be served. Let's face it; many highly educated professors view it as a professional comedown to "serve" 18 year old "know-nothing" students. Professors who would rather be served by students are likely to be poor teachers compared to those who see it as their duty to serve students.

Couple that with the many problems that exist in higher education with respect to teaching: cost, quality, value, graduation rate, etc. If faculty cannot accept students as customers, then it is unlikely that problems associated with teaching – the core mission of colleges and universities – will be recognized and corrected.

The inability to accept students as customer in higher education is an interesting problem that perhaps can be solved by looking to the field of mathematics. It is reminiscent of the long-ago fight among mathematicians who resisted the idea of imaginary numbers (e.g. $3i$, whose square is -9). Complex numbers, the correct term for imaginary numbers, were not widely accepted by mathematicians until the late 1700s – nearly 1700 years after they were conceived.

Negative numbers were an abstraction up to the middle 1500s. It made intuitive sense to have 3 apples, but it did not make sense to have -3 apples. What does it mean to have -3 apples? You have 3 apples or no apples, but not -3 apples. Once mathematicians began to accept the idea of imaginary numbers, it enabled them to solve important real-world problems that they could not otherwise solve, or solve important problems in simpler ways (i.e. polynomials).

So it is with students as "customers." Thinking of students as imaginary customers, C_i, is useful for solving important real-world problems in higher education or making those problems easier to solve: cost, quality, value, graduation rate, etc. (see Appendix III).

Professors invariably think of "customer" in the context of consumption and commercial transactions, which they abhor because they comprehend the university as something other than a business. Consumption and commercial transactions are concrete contexts that our minds immediately default to. But, customer can also be used to denote attitudes and desires – abstract contexts that we are much less familiar with. Yet, this would help us comprehend what humans – students – want and focus our efforts on providing that.

Automatic reversion to the concrete context of "customer" is an excuse to preserve the status quo and ignore the need to recognize and correct problems. This leaves professors stuck in the past, wedded to ineffective pedagogies, mistake-filled teaching, students who forget what they learned the moment the last class is ends, and so on.

We can think of students as partners, empowered learners, and producers and keep teaching as we have always done, or we can think of students as imaginary customers, C_i, and get on with the work of solving important real-world problems in higher education and fulfill our role as professors who serve students.

Let's hope it does not take another 700-plus years since the founding of University of Bologna in 1088 for C_i to be widely accepted by academics in higher education.

Source: http://www.leanprofessor.com/2015/01/13/imaginary-customers/

Appendix II

Questions and Answers

Here are some questions I have received over the years from professors and my answers. I hope you find them helpful.

Question 1: Most of your recommendations hold for class sizes of no more than 25 or so. Any (Lean) suggestions/ideas for handling a 300+ size class, where student noise and disturbances are most distressing [to] me as a teacher trying to get something important into the heads?

Answer: You are correct. My focus is class sizes of up to 40 or so students. You will have to apply Lean thinking to your problem and do some experiments to determine if actual improvement has occurred. Here are a few suggestions:

Large batch sizes exist for the producer's benefit, not for the customer's benefit. Therefore, you must reduce the batch size of 300+ to something much smaller. Do that in steps, if needed.

Perhaps this is a good place for technology to help. Use recorded video lectures to eliminate the large lecture hall setting and use class time to meet with students to discuss or explain things. A population of students, perhaps up to 25 percent, will prefer being taught this way. This will help reduce the batch size of face-to-face students in the classroom.

Run the course half in the lecture hall and half online.
Educate students on the "Respect for People" principle to address student noise/disturbances. Give examples of the many dimensions of RP, including discourteous noises and disturbances.

Question 2: Do you assign any of the books you have written to students for the courses that you teach?

Answer: I have done so in the past, but not since 2006 (*Better Thinking, Better Results* was assigned as required reading for my Lean Leadership course ca. 2003-2006). The books are neither required nor recommended reading in any of my courses because I do not want any conflicts of interest. Students can make independent judgments if they want to buy my books.

Other professors use my books, mainly for graduate courses in management, technology management, engineering management, etc. They use *Better Thinking, Better Results*, and, to a lesser extent *REAL LEAN, Volume One*. The intended audience for my books is senior managers, not academics or their students (unless the students are in an executive education program). These two books seem to work fairly well in graduate courses.

Question 3: OK, it's excellent. But how do I get started?

Answer: Great! I'm happy to hear you are getting started. You can begin by documenting the primary learning objectives of the course, based on the main subject matter. Think about this without looking at any books or other reference material. Then break that up into a logical, week-by-week sequence. This will help you create weekly homework assignments, in-class exercises, the end-of-course student visual control, etc. Then, write and edit the syllabus, as this represents the overall structure, content, and timing of the course.

The chapters in textbooks may be helpful in figuring out the primary learning objectives of the course, but don't let the book anchor you into a structure or sequence that does not make sense. Think critically about the content: What are the most 3-5 important things that students must know and be able to apply in the real world? This will evolve over time. Example: One of the most important things to learn in an operations management course is one-piece flow and how flow is achieved (the principles and practices that enable continuous flow). Then, figure out how to teach this and the (vital few) other important things over a 12 week semester.

You must constantly scrutinize the course content, timing, and delivery in relation to student's reaction to them and the learning outcomes you have identified (which will change over time). You will never be "done" with the course. You will continuously improve it in real-time and at the end of each semester. And, you will do so always with Lean principles and practices in mind. You will ask:

- "Is this an improvement? How does it eliminate waste, unevenness, or unreasonableness?"

- "Is this consistent with the 'Respect for People' principle? How so?"

- "How does set-up reduction apply to teaching?"

- "How else can I apply the Just-in-Time concept to teaching?"

- "How would an andon cord be used in teaching?"

- "What visual controls can I create to convey important information at-a-glance?"

- "How can I mistake-proof this assignment to reduce the errors that students make and to better ensue the desired learning outcomes are achieved?"

Question 4: I looked at your undergraduate course syllabus. Could you tell me more about in-class group cases?

Answer: The in-class group cases for the undergraduate course consist of one or more vignettes of a problem, typically a paragraph or two, that students read, discuss, and answer in 15 to 30 minutes. I write the vignettes myself, based on my work experience in industry, or borrow from other sources (with attribution) and edit them to suit my needs and the desired learning outcome.

Question 5: How do you grade in-class group cases?

Answer: Each in-class group assignment is worth 1, 2, or 3 points, depending upon the course. For example, they are graded as: 2 = on-target, 1 = somewhat off-target, 0 = totally off-target (and thus an opportunity for me to improve [mistake-proof] the in-class group case). Immediately after the case is turned in to me, I explain to students the solutions that would have been on-target, somewhat off- target, and totally off-target.

Question 6: What do you include in course packets for homework reading?

Answer: The reading material is collected from a variety of sources and consists of magazine articles, newspaper articles, essays that I have written, and peer-reviewed journal papers, depending on the course. I assemble them into a reading pack, which undergoes a lot of changes each semester to ensure the reading material is both current and relevant to that week's topic. (See Chapter 3, Note 5).

Question 7: Are the weekly assignments that you ask students to turn in based on the readings they do before class? Are you gauging them for how much they understood from the readings?

Answer: Yes. Homework assignments are typically one, a few, or several questions from each week's reading material (typically qualitative, given the courses that I teach). I grade students based on whether or not they answered the questions correctly, which means that I am also gauging what they understood from the readings. I then review the homework details and learning outcome in class the next day. The idea behind the weekly graded homework assignments is to focus students on answering one or more very specific question and channel their work into a very specific learning outcome. Sometimes the "answer" to the question is simply data that I collect from students and then create charts or graphs to discuss in class the next day and elaborate on the learning outcome. Other times, students are asked to extrapolate the reading to a different situation and answer questions in a different topic area.

Appendix II   113

Question 8: It is a scary thought to not have exams. Would students take me for being too easy? I am not sure about the repercussions of not having exams in my class. Any suggestions?

Answer: This is a great opportunity to be creative! Think about alternative forms of evaluation that would be appropriate (as well as lower stress than in-class exams). You will have to experiment with this over time. I find that student learning greatly increases when the threat of mid-term exams, final exams, and pop quizzes are eliminated. At first, they will think you're nuts, or too easy, but soon they will realize that you are much more serious about learning, retention, and real-world practice than testing. I am not sure about any repercussions that you might face. Check your university policy to see if exams are actually required. The university registrar's mid-term and final exam schedule does not constitute a requirement for faculty to give these exams. Usually, in-class exams are not required, but some form of student evaluation is usually need – though still perhaps not required.

Question 9: I don't think our students would like me to shift from the mid-term and final exam structure we have always used to a weekly graded assignment structure. What kind of resistance have you faced from students?

Answer: I have faced virtually no resistance. Students prefer to have the work and graded assignments level-loaded, and they learn more as a result of this structure. Occasionally, a student will give me feedback that they would have learned more in the course if I gave mid-term and final exam. My response to this is two-fold: Firstly, the student has been conditioned over many years that learning is best achieved by mid-term and final exams. I do not believe this is true because people who do well in exams often fail (in various ways) in their duties at work (i.e. they did not actually learn the material). Secondly, I include in all of my syllabi the following statement: "These are minimum course requirements. If you feel you would get more out of this course through tests, projects, term papers, etc., please let me know." I've never had any takers.

Overall, I have found students to be generous in their willingness to be active participants in my efforts to experiment and develop the Lean teaching pedagogy over the last 15 years. The reaction isn't, "No, don't do that! We love the status quo." Instead, it is, "Finally! A professor is thinking about how to do things differently and is serious about improving."

In my view, one of the things that hurts student learning and their higher education experience is the continued use by faculty of the pedagogies and routines used in K-12 education. Why do that?

Question 10: How do you evaluate weekly graded assignments when you have 300 students in a class?

Answer: One way to do that would be borrow a few Lean concepts such as single-point learning lessons and go/no-go plug gauges. Whether you have 30 or 300 students, the idea is assure that the weekly graded assignment is focused on a single point (or perhaps two points) and that the work submitted is satisfactory and can be evaluated almost at-a-glance.

To make this work, students have to be informed that satisfactory work may not warrant individual feedback. Unsatisfactory work will warrant feedback, but if the instructor has mistake-proofed the assignment, then there should be few instances of unsatisfactory work. The instructor should, of course, always give group feedback, emphasizing the overall outcome of the assignment, relevancy to the topic, and relevancy to students' lives or careers.

The point of higher education is learning, not "mastery," as some say. Therefore, single-point learning lessons and go/no-go grading gauges should be sufficient in most cases (especially in graduate studies).

Question 11: I am a huge fan of the weekly assignments (thanks to you!) and have been successful in other regular courses where I teach in all the classes. The way my new class is designed is that for most of the lectures I have guest speakers come speak and share their perspective with the students. I am quite unsure what the weekly assignments should be. What ideas do you have?

Answer: The problem with guest lectures is that it can be like a class without having to think - a mental field trip where students just listen to information but no demand is placed upon them by the professor to then process the information. Here's what I do: I give students a handout to take notes on that asks specific questions. I then can collect these (returning them to the students later) and use students' notes answers to formulate weekly homework assignments. The assignments are of a general nature pertaining to the subject, but not specific to the lecturer. That gets the ball rolling, which leads to other types of weekly assignments.

Question 12: If you had to design a course from the start, how would you do it?

Answer: One thing that might help would be to create a course blueprint, similar to way a blueprint is created to define a manufactured part before it is produced.

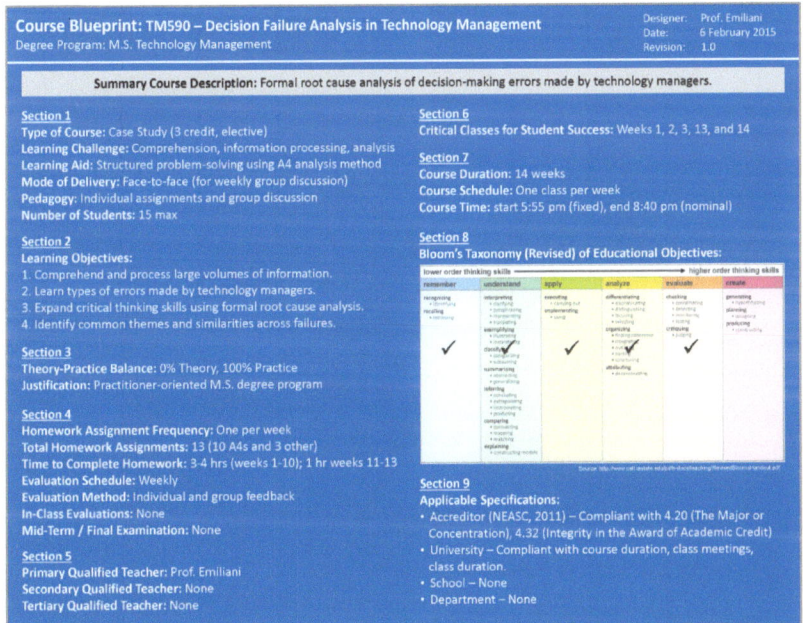

Appendix III

Teaching Survey Findings

Higher education leaders, like any other leader, mistakenly assume that processes central to their mission function well simply because they function. They are either unaware or deny that basic academic processes have serious problems – problems so serious that they negatively impact students' experience and their (and payers') perception of value. Admitting this truth, they think, will make them look weak and inept.

In contrast, a Lean leader knows that in a conventionally managed college or university, core academic processes are filled with waste, unevenness, and unreasonableness due to the pervasiveness of batch-and- queue processing. In Lean, revealing the truth makes leaders look strong and capable. That is why organizations need Lean leaders. They embrace problems, rather than ignore or hide them.

Over the years, I have been involved in numerous lines of research pertaining to different aspects of Lean management and Lean leadership. I have recently shifted my attention to correcting two fundamental, intertwined problems in higher education:

> 45 Teaching Errors
> The 10 Percent Problem

I have asked hundreds of graduates from schools around the world this question:

> "Of the 40 or so professors you had as an undergraduate, how many were really good?"

The answer is always the same: three or four (10 percent). Based on my experience, this is no anecdote. Higher education leaders who are data-driven, and thus ignore qualitative data, will allow this problem to linger for decades, as has been the case. Lean leaders do not ignore qualitative data.

Why are only 10 percent of professors remembered by students as having been really good? Were the other professors that bad, or merely forgettable as a result of average teaching abilities? Is the response personality-driven or an accurate reflection of the quality of instruction? My feeling is that the former plays a largely insignificant role, while the latter is the driver. Think about it: An education that requires 40 points of contact for weeks at a time and results in satisfaction with only 10 percent of the teachers is in dire need of rapid improvement. What is causing this problem?

Below is an Ishikawa diagram I created to show some of the possible secondary causes that contribute to the observed effect. While more work is needed to identify tertiary, quaternary, etc., causes, this diagram is a start towards developing a better understanding of the problem. Foremost, it suggests that the problem (effect) has multiple causes. So, there will be a lot of work to do to understand and correct the many problems that exist.

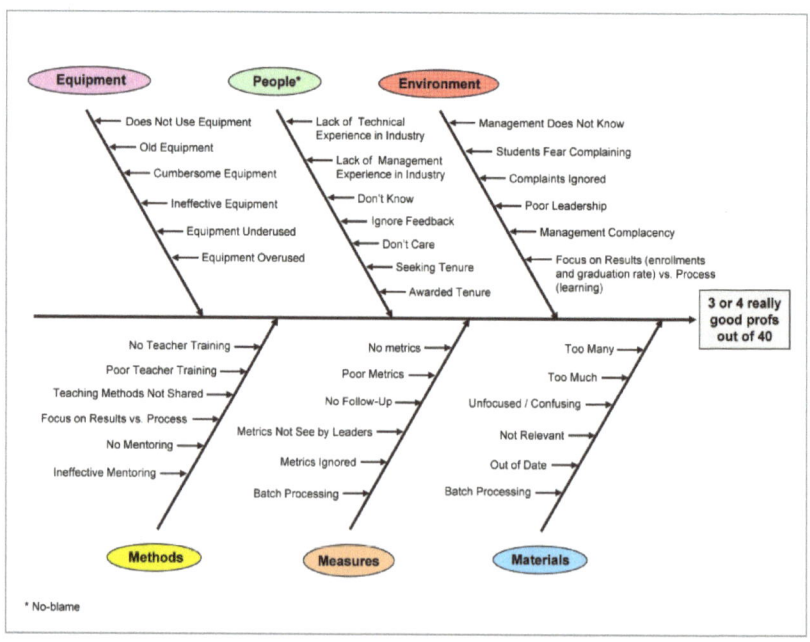

While both of my books, *Lean Teaching* and *Lean University*, seek to correct these problems, more data is needed to better understand them so that practical countermeasures can be applied.

I recently created two online surveys to capture data designed to identify which of the 45 teaching errors are most prevalent and the causes of the 10 percent problem. Surveys were completed by people who have completed an undergraduate degree, with an estimated response rate of about nine percent.

The charts for the 45 teaching errors are based on 123 responses, while the charts for the 10 percent problem are based on 137 responses recorded in two separate Google Docs spreadsheets from 18 June to 6 December 2013.

All charts were prepared by Kamna Tiwari, a graduate student in the Technology Management program at Central Connecticut State University.

45 Teaching Errors

For the 45 teaching errors, survey participants were asked one question: "Check the box for the teaching errors that you experienced as an undergraduate student in higher education."
The first chart shows the overall results.

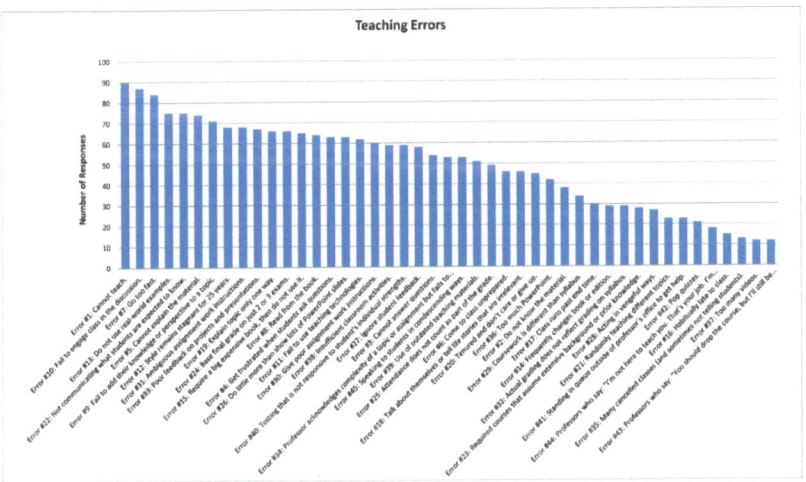

The distribution of the data shows that teaching errors do not follow an 80-20 rule. Instead of 80 percent of the responses coming from 20 percent of the errors (n = 9), 80 percent of the responses come from 60 percent of the errors (n = 28).

This suggests that students experience numerous teaching errors from each instructor they had as an undergraduate. This cannot be a source of satisfaction for students. Rather, it is a source of dissatisfaction that students talk about among themselves, with their parents, and others – expect, apparently, top university administrators. Could this be a significant driver of the 10 percent problem? Recall our simple definition for quality in teaching from Chapter 2:

"Quality is the absence of known or obvious teaching errors."

The next chart shows the top 15 known and obvious teaching errors, according to survey respondents.

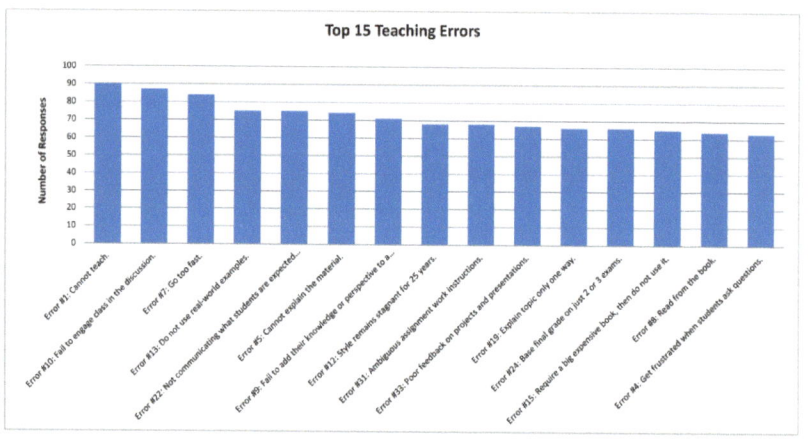

The top 15 errors shown in the chart are:

Error #1   Cannot teach.
Error #10 Fail to engage class in the discussion.
Error #7   Go too fast.
Error #13 Do not use real-world examples.
Error #22 Not communicating what students are expected

		to know.
Error	#5	Cannot explain the material.
Error	#9	Fail to add their knowledge or perspective to a topic.
Error	#12	Style remains stagnant for 25 years.
Error	#31	Ambiguous assignment work instructions.
Error	#33	Poor feedback on projects and presentations.
Error	#19	Explain topic only one way.
Error	#24	Base final grade on just 2 or 3 exams.
Error	#15	Require a big expensive book, then do not use it.
Error	#8	Read from the book.
Error	#4	Get frustrated when students ask questions.

These are remarkable results. I'd like to comment on the top 5 errors:

Error #1 Cannot teach.

How can that be? Well, being a professor does not mean one can teach, just as being a university president does not mean one can lead. Professionalism in a given discipline requires deep study and practice. In most cases, practice is abundant but the study of teaching (and leadership) is missing.

Error #10 Fail to engage class in the discussion.

Lecturing without asking for or soliciting questions from students suggests faculty want to be done with each class as soon as possible and with the least amount of effort. This error is closely connected to Error #7.

Error #7 Go too fast.

Most courses are over-contented. Taking out some material will help teachers slow down. Ask: "What are the 5 most important things that students should know from this course?"

Error #13 Do not use real-world examples.

Why not? Perhaps is it because a lack of industry work experience makes the real world seem abstract and irrelevant to faculty. Yet real-world examples are what students want, whether in arts or sciences.

Error #22 Not communicating what students are expected to know.

One can consider faculty as educational supervisors to students. A basic error that most supervisors make is failing to establish expectations. Students may not like what they hear, but at least they will know what is expected of them.

The clear message from this data is that there should be a determined focus by individual faculty and by institutional leadership to eliminate the 45 teaching errors. The way to do this is by improving teaching processes.

Eliminating these errors will end the end the "cycle of abuse" improve the value proposition of higher education for students, payers, employers, and others.

Cycle of Abuse in Higher Education

The 10 Percent Problem

For the 10 percent problem survey, participants were asked one question: "Identify what you consider to be the top driver of the observed effect for each of the six categories of the above fishbone diagram."

The next six charts show the results for the 10 percent problem survey by the major cause categories shown in the fishbone diagram: Environment, People, Equipment, Materials, Measures, and Methods.

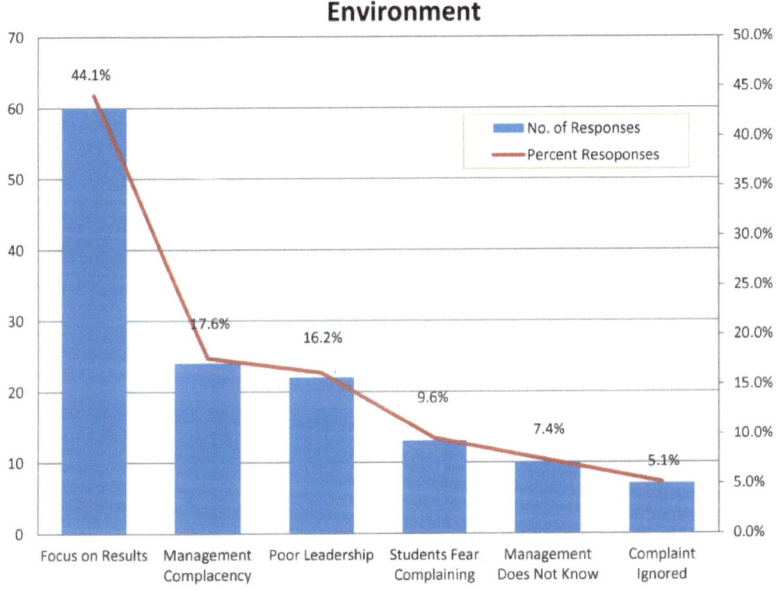

The category "Environment" means the overall university environment with respect to its priorities. On the survey form, "Focus on Results" was presented as: "Focus on Results (enrollments and graduation rate) vs. Process (learning)." Thus, survey respondents felt that the focus on results, which, of course, is driven by top administrators, is the primary driver of the 10 percent problem for the "Environment" cause category.

Note that administrators today are more strongly focused on results – enrollments and graduation rate – than in previous years. This is due to declining enrollments (particularly in small private and public higher education) and political pressure to improve graduation rates. It suggests that teaching will continue to fall below students' expectations in the future because improving teaching is not the primary focus of higher education leaders.

The remaining items shown in the chart suggests poor leadership and an environment where administrators are unwilling to listen to students or are ignorant of what is happening with respect to students' interests. This is no surprise to those who are familiar with conventional (non-Lean) leadership mindset and practices.

The category "People" comes next. On the survey form, "People" was presented as: "People (professors -- no-blame)." This wording was used to inform survey participants not to blame people (faculty) for observed effect, but to recognize that people play a role in any process.

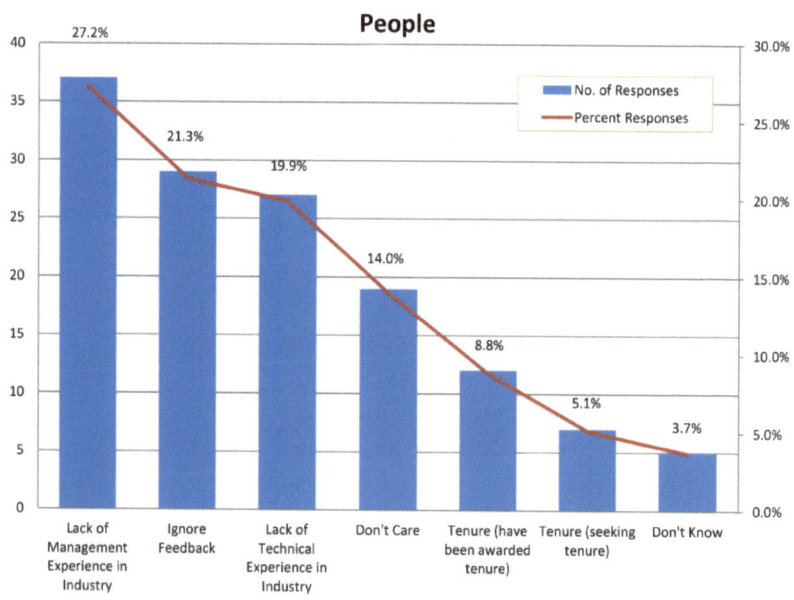

The top "People" cause is "Lack of Management Experience," while the third cause is "Lack of Technical Experience in Industry." Survey respondents indicate that teachers who lack industry experience are not as good at teaching as those who do have management and technical work experience in industry. Education would be of greater value to students if more professors had spent time in the types of work environments that students will eventually occupy.

The relationship of this to the observed effect is the result of low value that institutions of higher education place on industry work experience as a prerequisite for teaching. It also reflects the hiring process for faculty, which strongly favors candidates with little or no industry work experience (see The Preface, Note 9).

Survey respondents see industry work experience as an asset that improves teaching. Faculty hiring processes currently do not, but should be improved to incorporate what students see as adding value to their educational experience.

Unfortunately, it appears that some faculty are adept at ignoring student feedback and generally do not seem to care about students to the extent that they say they do.

The category "Equipment" comes next. On the survey form, "Equipment" was presented as: "Equipment (includes software, learning management systems, and related technologies)." The major responses are: "Ineffective Equipment," Equipment Underused," and Does Not Use Equipment."

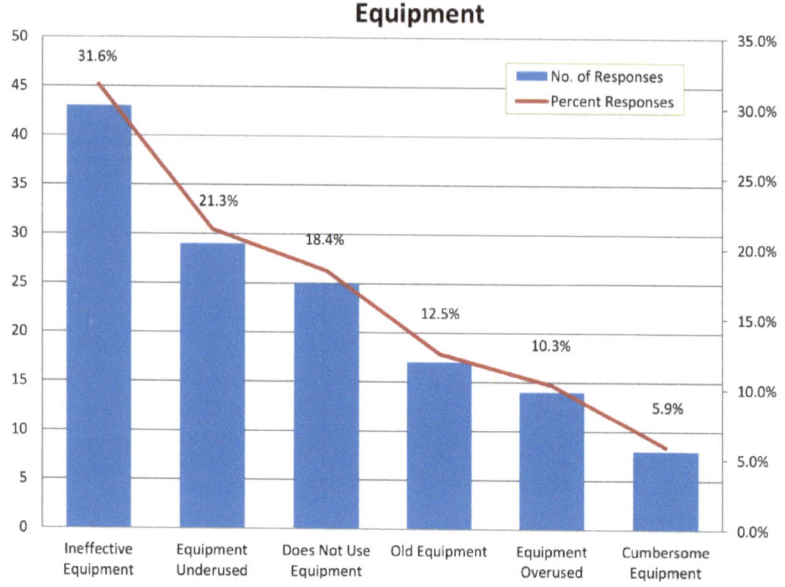

One can infer from these results a lack of training for faculty in how to use the equipment; the purchase of inferior, unnecessary, or difficult to use equipment by administrators; or faculty unwillingness to use new equipment.

In Lean, we carefully consider whether new equipment is actually necessary to do a job. Manual processing can be OK. New equipment is not purchased just for the sake of having new equipment. If equipment is needed, then only the necessary features are procured. This helps reduce costs and assure that people will actually use the equipment or technology. And, to be consistent with the "Respect for People" principle, equipment or technology must serve people – not the other way around.

The category "Material" comes next. On the survey form, "Material" was presented as: "Materials (used in teaching)." The results indicate that the biggest problem is teacher's use of unfocused and confusing teaching materials.

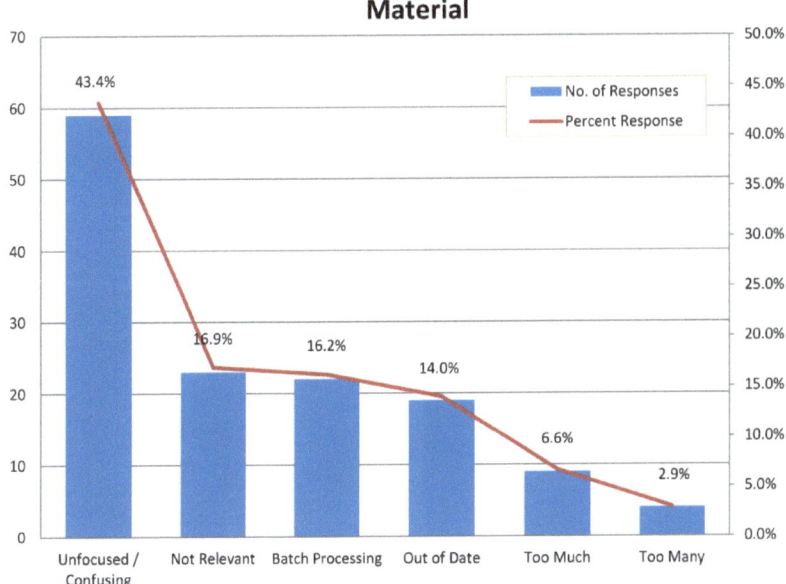

The kaizens I led at Rensselaer showed this to be the case for every one of the 10 courses in the Executive Master's Program, including teaching materials that were not relevant or were out of date. From the professor's perspective, all teaching materials used in a course have a clear place and a clear purpose. To them, it all makes sense. But, it does not make sense to survey respondents. Professors create courses in isolation, and, as a result, accidentally introduce too much or confusing teaching materials. The lack of peer review in the process of creating and updating courses accounts for this result.

The item "Batch Processing" reflects the batch processing nature of students' assignments that use the teaching materials (e.g. term papers, mid-term or final exams, etc.).

The category "Measures" comes next. On the survey form, "Measures" was presented as: "Measures (pertaining to teaching)." Survey respondents seem to feel that the 10 percent problem is partly caused by using metrics that are poor in their ability to discriminate between good teaching and poor teaching. The next category suggests that whatever the metric(s) used, good or bad, the result is unlikely to be acted upon by faculty (or administrators).

Some survey respondents thought that teaching metrics did not exist, or that the teaching metrics of individual faculty were not reviewed by top administrators.

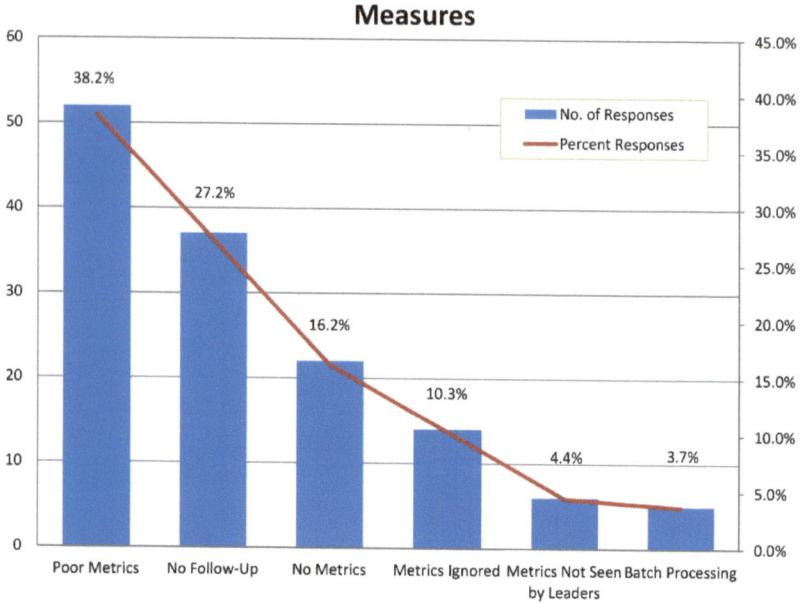

The final category, "Methods," comes next. On the survey form, "Methods" was presented as: "Methods (related to developing teaching skills)." Survey respondents indicate that the result of having taught a course is more important than the process to teach a course well.

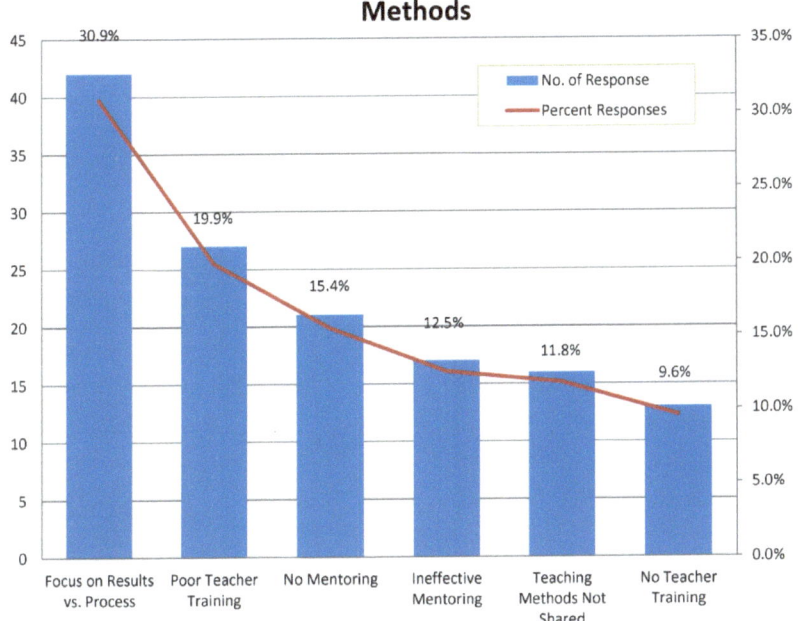

Whether fact or perception, poor teacher training, a lack of mentoring, ineffective mentoring, teaching methods not shared, and no teacher training should not be the characteristics of organizations that exist for the purpose of educating people.

The six charts shows the top drivers of the 10 percent problem are:

- Focus on Results (enrollments and graduation rate)
- Lack of Management Experience in Industry
- Ineffective Equipment
- Unfocused/Confusing (teaching materials)
- Poor (teaching) Metrics
- Focus on Results (teach the course) vs. Process (how to teach well).

Efforts to improve teaching, therefore, should begin with these, and the preferred process for doing that is kaizen. Recall the three principles of kaizen from Chapter 1:

- Process and results
- System focus
- Non-blaming, non-judgmental

The charts and analyses represent preliminary data and preliminary findings, and they are subject to the limitations of Internet survey research. Nevertheless, the findings resonate with what I have experienced. I suspect the same is true for you as well.

The shape of the charts may change a bit over time as more data accumulates, but the trends seem representative of actual conditions as they have existed for many decades in most institutions. Despite limitations, the findings are helpful because they suggest specific areas to target for process improvement, by individual faculty or by institutions as a whole.

Recall what I said in the Introduction:

"Professors can either wait for administrators to discover a better way, or they can begin without them. I recommend that faculty begin without them. Students, employers, and other important stakeholders are waiting for professors to improve, so let's start now."

Yes, let's start now. Every student deserves to experience better teaching. Working individually, we can turn the 10 percent problem into the 50 percent problem. With great university leadership, we can do even better.

About the Author

M.L. "Bob" Emiliani is a professor in the School of Engineering, Science, and Technology at Connecticut State University in New Britain, Conn., where he teaches courses on Lean management and a unique course that analyzes failures in management decision-making.

Bob holds a bachelor's degree in mechanical engineering from the University of Miami, a master's degree in chemical engineering from the University of Rhode Island, and a Ph.D. degree in Engineering from Brown University.

He worked in the consumer products and aerospace industries for 15 years, beginning as a materials engineer. He has held management positions in engineering, manufacturing, and supply chain management, and had responsibility for implementing Lean in manufacturing and supply chains at Pratt & Whitney.

Bob joined academia in September 1999 at Rensselaer Polytechnic Institute (Hartford, Connecticut campus) and worked there until 2004. He has applied Lean principles and practices to the courses he teaches since he joined academia, and led the first kaizens to improve an accredited master's degree program in 2002-2003. He joined Connecticut State University in 2005.

Emiliani has authored or co-authored 19 books, four book chapters, over 35 peer-reviewed papers on Lean management and related topics, and 10 papers on materials science and engineering. He has received six awards for writing.

Bob served as the North American regional editor for *Supply Chain Management: An International Journal*, 2005-2007 and on the editorial review boards of *Leadership and Organization Development Journal*, 2006-2011, *Supply Chain Management: An International Journal*, 2001-

2011, *Management Decision*, 2001-2011, and *Industrial Marketing Management*, 2005-2009.

He has been an ad-hoc reviewer for *Journal of Management History, Journal of Management Development, International Journal of Operations and Production Management, International Journal of Marketing for Industrial and High Tech Firms, Journal of Marketing Research, International Journal of Electronic Business,* and *Quality Assurance in Education.*

Please visit my web sites:
- www.leanprofessor.com
- www.profemiliani.net
- www.bobemiliani.com

www.ingramcontent.com/pod-product-compliance
Lightning Source LLC
Chambersburg PA
CBHW041622220426
43662CB00001B/13